200 fab fish dishes

W9-BNK-568

200 fab fish dishes

hamlyn **all color**

Gee Charman

An Hachette UK Company
www.hachette.co.uk

First published in Great Britain in 2009 by Hamlyn,
a division of Octopus Publishing Group Ltd
2–4 Heron Quays, London E14 4JP
www.octopusbooksusa.com

Some of the recipes in this book have previously appeared
in other books published by Hamlyn.

ISBN: 978-0-600-62016-7

A CIP catalog record for this book is available from the
Library of Congress

Printed and bound in China

1 2 3 4 5 6 7 8 9 10

Standard level spoon measurements are used in all recipes.

Ovens should be preheated to the specified temperature
—if using a fan-assisted oven, follow the manufacturer's
instructions for adjusting the time and the temperature.

Fresh herbs should be used unless otherwise stated.

Medium eggs should be used unless otherwise stated.

The Food and Drug Administration advises that eggs should
not be consumed raw. This book contains some dishes made
with raw or lightly cooked eggs. It is prudent for vulnerable
people such as pregnant and nursing mothers, invalids, the
elderly, babies, and young children to avoid uncooked or lightly
cooked dishes made with eggs. Once prepared, these dishes
should be kept refrigerated and used promptly.

This book includes dishes made with nuts and nut
derivatives. It is advisable for those with known allergic
reactions to nuts and nut derivatives and those who may be
potentially vulnerable to these allergies, such as pregnant and
nursing mothers, invalids, the elderly, babies, and children, to
avoid dishes made with nuts and nut oils. It is also prudent to
check the labels of pre-prepared ingredients for the possible
inclusion of nut derivatives.

contents

introduction

introduction

Fish is the original fast food. It is quick to prepare and cook, and with so many different types of fish and shellfish on the market you could eat a different type every night for over a month.

The fish used in the recipes of this book can easily be changed for other similar fish. The general rule is to try and get the same type of fish if the one stated is not your favorite or is unavailable. White-fleshed, round fish, such as sea bass, can be replaced by goatfish or mullet. Instead of flat fish, such as flounder, you can use bream, Dover sole, or lemon sole. Smaller shrimp can be changed for jumbo shrimp, cockles for mussels or clams, and salmon for trout.

Most of the recipes are quick to prepare and cook, although some require a little advanced planning for marinating or slow cooking. However, the actual amount of time you will be in the kitchen is never that long and the results will be delicious.

There are six chapters in the book—nibbles, soups and stews, salads and appetizers, pastas, legumes, and grains, main courses, and barbecue—and the quantities in many of these recipes can be changed to make the nibbles an appetizer or the appetizers a main course, for example. The barbecue recipes could also be adapted for less-good weather by using a broiler, an oven, or a really hot skillet.

Buying fish and shellfish

There are a few key points that should be followed when buying fish and shellfish. In all cases, always buy it fresh, as the fresher the fish the better the flavor and texture. It is easiest to tell how fresh whole fish are by looking at them. Whole fish should have bright, clear eyes, ruby-red gills, a clear slime covering the fish, and, most importantly, they should not smell "fishy." Fresh fish smells of the sea and not of fish!

With fish that has already been filleted, it is a little more difficult to judge how fresh it is, but the flesh should be firm and the skin bright, and it should smell of the sea.

The freshness of shellfish is very important, so always ask your fish merchant when it was caught. It should be no more than a day old, or two at the very most. Again, there should be no strong smell of fish.

Mussels, clams, and cockles should be bought and cooked live. Many supermarkets sell these types of shellfish in vacuum-sealed packs, which suffocate them. These should be avoided if at all possible.

Ethical sourcing of fish

For many years the seas around the world have been overfished, with different species being affected at different times as popularity fluctuates with fashions and trends. Unfortunately, the consequence of

FOR RECIPES USING	YOU COULD ALSO TRY...
ANCHOVIES	Smelt • Sardines • Whitebait
ANGLER FISH	Cod
CLAMS	Mussels • Oysters • Cockles • Razor Clams
COD	Pollock • Hoki • Haddock • Hake • Whiting (large)
CRAYFISH	Lobsterette • Shrimp (jumbo)
FLOUNDER	Dover Sole • Lemon Sole
HADDOCK, SMOKED	Kippers • Smoked Cod
HAKE	Cod
HALIBUT	Brill • Turbot
HERRINGS	Mackerel • Sardines
MACKEREL	Sardines • Herrings
MACKEREL, SMOKED	Smoked Eel • Smoked Salmon • Smoked Trout
PERCH	Salmon • Trout
RED MULLET	Tilapia • Sea Bream • Sea Bass
RED SNAPPER	Sea Bream • Goatfish • Red Bream • Mullet
SALMON	Trout • Salmon Trout • Steelhead Trout
SARDINES	Herrings • Mackerel (small)
SEA BASS	John Dory • Brill • Flounder • Sole
SEA BREAM	Red Bream • Goatfish • Red Snapper • Mullet
SHRIMP	Scallops • Langoustine (Dublin Bay Prawns) • Scampi
SQUID (CALAMARI, INKFISH)	Cuttlefish • Octopus
SWORDFISH	Ray • Shark • Tuna
TROUT, SMOKED	Smoked Mackerel • Smoked Eel
TUNA	Shark • Swordfish • Bonito • Mahi Mahi
TURBOT	Halibut • Brill • Sole

overfishing still affects the world's waters today. New laws are now in place in most countries to try to prevent this from happening again and to allow diminished stocks to recover. In addition, careless fishing, in which unwanted sea creatures are caught in the fishing nets often to die in the water, or are hauled up onto the decks only to be tossed back into the sea as waste, is having an impact on fish stocks, as well as being cruel. Make sure, therefore, that you always buy dolphin-friendly tuna.

It is now vital that consumers take matters into their own hands and check that the fish they are buying is ethically and sustainably sourced. If you don't know where the fish you are buying has come from, then don't buy it. There are so many alternatives (see chart, opposite) and good-quality farmed fish is now so widely available, that we can easily allow our natural stock to replenish. There are many web sites that will tell you which fish are endangered in certain waters from around the world and which species are safe to buy, making it easier to buy ethically.

Farmed fish is obviously an ethical way of sourcing certain types of fish, but it has had a bad press over the years due to the overcrowding of sea cages, especially in the case of salmon farming. If you are buying farmed fish, try to buy organic, as the cages tend to be less densely stocked and no chemicals are used, which is better for our health. Look for government recognition on the pack of farmed fish to ensure high standards of husbandry.

Storing fish

Fish should be kept for only 1–2 days in the refrigerator. The refrigerator temperature should be between 34°F and 41°F. Fish should be removed from any packaging and placed on a clean plate, covered with a clean, damp cloth and then loosely covered with plastic wrap. The same method should be used for scallops and shrimp.

Mussels, clams, and cockles are difficult to keep alive, as they are easily suffocated. The best way, if you are storing the shellfish overnight, is to place them in a colander with a few ice cubes or ice flakes set over a bowl in the refrigerator. Keep topping up the ice as it melts.

Fresh fish can be frozen, although freezing does change the flavor and texture a little. If you want to freeze your own fish, make sure you buy it as fresh as possible. Wrap it up in plastic wrap and place it in a sealable plastic bag or airtight container (which will reduce the likelihood of freezer burn), then place it in the freezer.

Allow frozen fish to thaw out in the refrigerator, preferably overnight, and once it has thawed, use that day. Thawed fish can be a little wet, so wipe it with paper towels before cooking to remove some of the excess moisture. Never refreeze thawed fish.

Preparing fish and shellfish

The preparation of fish, especially gutting and scaling, can be messy, so ask your fish merchant to do it for you, along with filleting.

Clams, mussels, and cockles that are bad are easily spotted. If they are open before cooking and don't close when tapped or do not open when cooked, discard them. Likewise for any that have broken shells. Rinse mussels, clams, and cockles under cold running water for a couple of minutes to remove some of the grit found in their shells.

Scallops are usually sold already cleaned by fish merchants: i.e. the white muscle and orange coral have already been removed from the shell. If you buy scallops still in their shells, you will need to remove the gills, which look like a feathery "skirt" around the edge. To do this, remove the whole scallop (muscle, coral, and skirt) from the shell by loosening the muscle with a sharp knife, then pull the skirt away from the muscle using your fingers.

Squid has a bad reputation, as it is often tough and rubbery, but that is because it has been cooked incorrectly. There is no middle ground when it comes to cooking squid: it should be very fast or very slow, and either method will result in beautifully tender squid. If cooking it quickly, you need to use a very, very hot pan and fry it for only a minute; alternatively, braise it slowly as though making a stew. Preparing squid is simpler than it looks, since it is bought part-prepared. Pull the tentacles out of the main body, where they will have been placed, and, if you want to use them, cut them from the head just below the eye. Now take the main sac or body, also known as a tube, and feel inside for a hard,

Mussels will generally need to be debearded at home. Simply pull the fibrous beards from the mussels. If they are a little stubborn, simply cut them off with a pair of scissors. Barnacles will also need to be scubbed off.

plastic-like quill. If one is there, pull it out and discard it. Now rinse the body out well, then either cut it down one side to open it out or just slice it into rings. If you are scoring the flesh to help tenderize it, always score the inside of the flesh.

Cooking fish

In most of the recipes in this book the fish takes only minutes to cook, and therefore it is important to get everything ready before it hits the pan. The most common mistake when cooking fish is to overcook it.

When pan-frying fillets of fish with the skin on, three-quarters of the cooking should be done on the skin side, as this protects the flesh and allows it to cook without becoming dry. You should be able to see that the fish is almost cooked, as it becomes opaque around the edges, before turning it over to cook the other side for a minute or so.

If you are unsure as to whether fish is cooked or not, insert the sharp point of a knife or a toothpick into the flesh. If it glides into the flesh easily, without resistance, then the fish is cooked. This is a handy tip when cooking thicker fillets or roasting fish. Cooked fish will also feel firm to the touch and be opaque in color.

Essential flavors

Even if you have no time to go shopping, a few pantry ingredients open up a whole world of flavors for quick and easy recipes from around the world. Dried ingredients such as pasta, legumes, and grains and sauces such

Thai fish sauce, soy sauce, sweet chili sauce, and harissa paste will all keep for months in the pantry and refrigerator, and will help to make wonderful dishes.

There is a huge variety of spices on the market now, and adding a few of the essentials can result in wonderful curries and spiced stews in minutes. Make sure you always have coriander seeds, cumin seeds, fennel seeds, mustard seeds, turmeric, garam masala, paprika, smoked paprika, and cayenne pepper in the cupboard. Red and green chilies freeze well for when you want to add a little more heat. Cans of tomatoes

and coconut milk are also essential for a quick curry or sauce. Cans and jars of olives, roasted peppers, sun-dried tomatoes, beans, and anchovies are other pantry essentials.

Flavored butters are a quick way to introduce flavors to fish that has been simply cooked. Make larger quantities than given in the recipes in this book and keep them in the freezer. Then simply cut a few slices from the roll of flavored butter and allow it to melt on the fish.

Nutritional value of fish

Many nutritionists recommend that you eat fish at least twice a week due to its nutritional benefits. Fish is naturally low in saturated fat and high in the essential fats, especially in the case of oily fish such as salmon and mackerel. These oily fish are high in omega-3, a fatty acid that must be ingested, as the body cannot naturally produce it. Omega-3 is an important part of the diet for both children and adults because it is necessary for a healthy nervous system.

Fish is also naturally high in protein, which is needed in every cell of the body to build healthy bones, muscles, tendons, and ligaments. There are also many vitamins, minerals, and trace elements found in fish, which contribute to a healthy and balanced diet. Shellfish can be high in cholesterol, but this type of cholesterol doesn't make a great contribution to your blood cholesterol levels, and so shellfish need not be avoided on health grounds.

making fish stock

Why bother making your own stock? In an age when we are all being advised to cut down on our salt consumption, homemade stock can be salt-free; it also fits in with our aspiration to recycle all we can.

Fish can be expensive, so if you have bought a whole fish that the fish merchant is going to fillet for you, ask to keep the bones and heads to make your own stock. (Note that flounder bones make a bitter stock and so are not worth keeping.)

If you haven't got time to make stock now, don't throw the fish bones out—just pack them into a plastic bag and freeze them until you do have time. The following recipe makes 4 cups.

If using frozen fish bones, make sure they are completely thawed before use. Don't try to speed up thawing by plunging them into warm water. Immerse in cold water and change the water frequently, or thaw in the microwave, following the manufacturer's guidelines. Stock can be frozen in ice cube trays then tipped into a bag and stored in the freezer for easy and convenient use.

Basic fish stock

1 lb leftover **fish bones**

6 cups water, or enough to cover the fish bones and vegetables

a few **vegetables**, such as **onion**, **celery**, **leek**, and **carrot**, roughly chopped

a few **peppercorns**

1 **bay leaf**

a few **thyme sprigs**

a few **parsley stalks**

salt and **pepper**

Cover the bones with the water and add the vegetables, peppercorns, bay leaf, thyme, and parsley. Bring the water to a boil, then reduce the heat and simmer for 20 minutes, removing any scum that comes to the surface.

Strain the stock, discarding the vegetables and bones, then place it over a high heat to reduce to the desired consistency and flavor.

Finally, season with salt and pepper.

nibbles

cured salmon & cucumber spoons

Serves **4**

Preparation time **15 minutes**,
  plus marinating

8 oz **skinless salmon fillet**,
  pin-boned and finely diced
4 tablespoons **lemon juice**
¼ **cucumber**, seeded and
  finely diced
2 tablespoons drained **capers**,
  finely chopped
1 tablespoon finely chopped
  tarragon
1 tablespoon **mayonnaise**
salt and **pepper**
a few **dill sprigs**, to garnish
  (optional)

Place the salmon in a nonmetallic bowl. Pour over
the lemon juice and toss the salmon in it until all the
pieces are coated. Cover and leave in the refrigerator
to marinate for 3 hours.

Drain off the excess lemon juice and discard. Mix
the salmon with the cucumber, capers, chopped
tarragon, and mayonnaise, season with salt and pepper,
and serve on silver or clear spoons topped with dill
sprigs, if desired.

For smoked salmon with pickled cucumber, using
a Y-shaped peeler, peel the outer flesh of a cucumber
into ribbons, leaving the seeds behind. In a small
saucepan, bring 2 tablespoons rice vinegar and
1 tablespoon superfine sugar to a boil. Remove from
the heat and allow to cool, then add to the cucumber
ribbons along with 1 tablespoon chopped dill weed.
Serve with smoked salmon.

sushi

Serves **4–6**

Preparation time **30 minutes**,
   plus cooling

Cooking time **15 minutes**

1 generous cup **sushi rice**

1¾ cups **water**

4 **scallions**, very finely
   shredded

4 tablespoons **seasoned rice
   vinegar**

1 tablespoon **superfine sugar**

1 oz **pickled ginger**, shredded

1 tablespoon **toasted sesame
   seeds**

3–4 **nori** sheets

4 oz very fresh **wild salmon**,
   sliced into small strips

1 large **skinless sole fillet**,
   pin-boned and sliced into
   small strips

10 **cooked peeled shrimp**

light soy sauce, to serve

Put the rice in a heavy saucepan with the measurement water. Bring slowly to a boil, then reduce the heat and simmer, half-covered, for 5–8 minutes, or until all the water has been absorbed. Cover completely and cook very gently for an additional 5 minutes, or until the rice is very tender and sticky. Turn into a bowl and leave to cool.

Stir the scallions, vinegar, sugar, ginger, and sesame seeds into the rice.

Use scissors to cut the nori sheets into 2½ inch squares. Dampen your hands and mold the rice into little ovals. Arrange the rice ovals diagonally over the nori squares.

Bring the pointed ends on opposite sides of the nori over the rice and arrange a piece of fish or a shrimp on top. Arrange on a serving platter and serve with a small bowl of soy sauce for dipping.

For chili & cilantro dipping sauce, to serve as an alternative accompaniment, place 4 tablespoons of light soy sauce in a bowl. Add 1 tablespoon sesame oil and a little wasabi paste and mix well. Add 1 finely chopped red chili, 1 teaspoon sesame seeds, and 1 tablespoon finely chopped cilantro leaves and stir well.

crisp fried seafood

Serves **4–6**
Preparation time **20 minutes**
Cooking time **5 minutes**

1 lb **mixed seafood**, such as
   smelt, skinned white fish, and
   squid, cleaned
   (see page 12)
1 **scallion**, finely chopped
1 **mild red chili**, seeded and
   thinly sliced
1 **garlic clove**, finely chopped
2 tablespoons chopped
   parsley
⅔ cup **semolina flour**
½ teaspoon **paprika**
sunflower oil, for deep-frying
salt and **pepper**
lemon or **lime wedges**,
   to serve

Cut the white fish into small chunks. Slice the squid into rings and pat dry on paper towels with the tentacles and any other seafood you might be using.

Mix the scallion with the chili, garlic, parsley, and some salt. Set aside.

Put the semolina flour and paprika on a plate and season lightly with salt and pepper. Add the seafood and coat well.

Pour the oil into a deep-fat fryer or large saucepan to a depth of at least 3 inches and heat to 350–375°F, or until a cube of bread browns in 30 seconds. Fry the fish in batches for 30–60 seconds until crisp and golden. Drain on paper towels and keep warm while you cook the remainder. Serve in little dishes, sprinkled with the scallion and herb mixture and accompanied by the lemon or lime wedges.

For sweet chili mayonnaise, to serve as an accompaniment, mix 4 tablespoons mayonnaise with 1 tablespoon sweet chili sauce. Squeeze the juice of ½ lemon into the mayonnaise and mix well. Add a little chopped chili if you like it hot.

thai-spiced shrimp toasts

Serves **4**

Preparation time **25 minutes**, plus cooling

Cooking time **20 minutes**

1 tablespoon **vegetable oil**

1 **onion**, finely chopped

1 **red chili**, seeded and finely chopped

2 inch piece of **fresh ginger root**, peeled and finely chopped

1 **garlic clove**, crushed

7 oz **raw peeled shrimp**

5 oz **ground pork**

1 **egg**, lightly beaten

1 tablespoon **Thai fish sauce**

2 tablespoons chopped **cilantro**, plus extra sprigs to garnish

finely grated zest of 2 **limes**

5 slices of **white bread**

2 tablespoons **sesame seeds**

vegetable oil, for deep-frying

salt and **pepper**

2 **limes**, cut into wedges, to garnish

Heat the oil in a skillet over a medium heat, add the onion, chili, and ginger and fry until the onion is soft. Add the garlic and fry for a minute more. Set aside to cool.

Place the cooled onion mixture, shrimp, and pork in a food processor and blend until a paste is formed. Add the egg, fish sauce, cilantro, lime zest, and a little salt and pepper and blend once more.

Spread this mixture over the bread in a layer about ½ inch thick. Sprinkle with the sesame seeds and cut into neat triangles.

Pour the oil into a deep-fat fryer or large saucepan to a depth of at least 3 inches and heat to 350–375°F, or until a cube of bread browns in 30 seconds. Fry the shrimp toasts in batches of 4 triangles at a time, shrimp-side down first, for 3 minutes, then turn over and cook on the bread side for a minute more. The shrimp toasts should be golden brown. Drain on paper towels and keep warm while you cook the remainder. Serve with lime slices to squeeze over the toasts, garnished with cilantro sprigs.

For lime & chili dipping sauce, to serve as an accompaniment, mix together 2 tablespoons lime juice, 2 tablespoons sweet chili sauce, and 2 tablespoons Thai fish sauce.

octopus with garlic dressing

Serves **6–8**

Preparation time **10 minutes**,
   plus cooling and chilling

Cooking time 1½ **hours**

1 **onion**, cut into wedges

1 teaspoon **whole cloves**

8 cups **water**

1 lb **prepared octopus**,
   bought at least 2 days before
   being cooked, and placed in
   the freezer for 48 hours to
   tenderize the meat

6 tablespoons **extra virgin
   olive oil**

2 **garlic cloves**, crushed

4 tablespoons chopped
   parsley

1 teaspoon **white wine
   vinegar**

salt and **pepper**

Put the onion, cloves, and 1 tablespoon salt in a large saucepan and add the measurement water. Bring to a boil. Using tongs, dip the octopus in and out of the water about 4 times, returning the water to a boil before re-dipping, then immerse the octopus completely in the water. (This helps to make the flesh tender.) If there are several pieces of octopus, dip them 1 at a time.

Reduce the heat and cook the octopus very gently for 1 hour, then check to see whether it's tender. Cook for an additional 15–30 minutes if necessary. Allow it to cool in the liquid, then drain, cut into bite-size pieces, and place in a nonmetallic bowl.

Mix the oil with the garlic, parsley, vinegar, and salt and pepper to taste and add to the bowl. Mix well, cover, and chill for several hours or overnight. Serve the octopus with bread for mopping up the juices.

For octopus with spicy chorizo, cook the octopus as above, then allow to cool; cut into bite-size pieces. Sprinkle 2 sliced chorizo sausages with 1 teaspoon sweet paprika and fry until crispy. Drain on paper towels to remove the excess oil. Place 2 tablespoons olive oil in a bowl with the juice of 1 lemon and the chorizo. Season with salt and pepper. Add the octopus and mix well to coat in the oil. When you are ready to serve, stir in 1 tablespoon chopped cilantro leaves and 1 tablespoon chopped parsley. Serve with bread.

salt cod pâté with crostini

Serves **4**

Preparation time **15 minutes**, plus soaking, cooling, and chilling

Cooking time **15 minutes**

10 oz pieces of **salt cod**
1 **garlic clove**, crushed
6 tablespoons **heavy cream**
½ teaspoon **paprika**
lemon juice, to taste
pepper
small bunch of **chives**, finely chopped, to garnish (optional)

Crostini
5 slices of **multigrain bread**
olive oil

Cover the salt cod in cold water and allow to soak for 12 hours, changing the water as often as possible.

Place the soaked salt cod in a saucepan and cover with fresh cold water. Bring to a boil, then reduce the heat and simmer for 5 minutes. Drain. When cool enough to handle, flake the fish into a food processor, removing the bones and skin. Add the garlic and blend. While the motor is running, pour in the cream. Remove from the processor and season with paprika, lemon juice, and pepper. Salt will most likely not be needed. Place the pâté in a bowl and cover with plastic wrap. Once cool, place in the refrigerator for at least 1 hour.

Make the crostini by stamping out 4 x 1¼ inch rounds from each slice of bread using a cookie or pastry cutter. Place them on a baking sheet, drizzle with a little olive oil, and cook for 7–10 minutes in a preheated oven, 350°F, until golden and crispy.

Spread the salt cod pâté on the crostini and sprinkle with finely chopped chives, if desired.

For salt cod with pepper salsa, soak and boil 10 oz salt cod as above. Once cooked, flake the fish into small pieces and fry in a little olive oil until crispy. Chop 7 oz mixed marinated peppers (from a jar) and mix with a little of their own oil. Add 8 drained and chopped sundried tomatoes in oil and 8 chopped pitted black olives. Serve the pepper mixture on little crostini, made as above, and top with a few flakes of salt cod and a squeeze of lemon.

salt & chili squid

Serves **6–8**

Preparation time **20 minutes**, plus chilling

Cooking time **3 minutes**

1½ lb **squid**, cleaned (see page 12) and halved lengthwise, tentacles discarded

¾ cup **lemon juice**

⅔ cup **cornstarch**

1½ tablespoons **salt**

2 teaspoons **white pepper**

1 teaspoon **chili powder**

2 teaspoons **superfine sugar**

4 **egg whites**, lightly beaten

sunflower oil, for deep-frying

Dipping sauce

1 **red chili**, seeded and finely diced

1 tablespoon diced **shallot**

2 teaspoons very finely chopped **cilantro**

6 tablespoons **light soy sauce**

1 tablespoon **Chinese rice wine**

To garnish

red chilies, seeded and finely sliced

scallions, finely sliced

Open the squid out and pat dry with paper towels. Lay them on a cutting board, shiny-side down, and, using a sharp knife, lightly score a fine diamond pattern on the flesh, being careful not to cut all the way through. Cut the squid into 2 x 1 inch pieces and place in a nonmetallic dish. Pour over the lemon juice, cover, and chill for 15 minutes.

Combine the cornstarch, salt, pepper, chili powder, and sugar in a bowl. Dip the squid pieces into the beaten egg whites and then into the cornstarch mixture, shaking off any excess.

Pour the oil into a deep-fat fryer or large saucepan to a depth of at least 3 inches and heat to 350–375°F, or until a cube of bread browns in 30 seconds. Deep-fry the squid in 3 batches for 1 minute, or until it turns pale golden and curls up. Remove each batch with a slotted spoon and drain on paper towels.

Mix all the ingredients for the dipping sauce in a bowl. Serve the squid in small paper cones, if desired, garnished with sliced red chili and scallions and accompanied by the dipping sauce.

For salt & pepper squid, prepare the squid as above. Mix together ⅔ cup cornstarch, 2 teaspoons superfine sugar, 1½ tablespoons salt, 1 teaspoon ground white pepper, and 1 teaspoon ground black pepper. Dip the squid into lightly beaten egg white and then into the cornstarch mixture. Deep-fry in sunflower oil for 1 minute, then drain on paper towels and serve as above.

spicy tuna skewers

Serves **4**

Preparation time **10 minutes**, plus marinating

Cooking time **6 minutes**

1 tablespoon **turmeric**

1 tablespoon **ground cumin**

1 tablespoon **ground coriander**

1½ inch piece of **fresh ginger root,** peeled and finely chopped

2 tablespoons **olive oil**

2 **garlic cloves,** crushed

13 oz **fresh tuna steak,** cut into chunks

¾ cup **plain yogurt**

finely grated zest of 1 **lemon**

vegetable oil, for brushing

salt and **pepper**

Put the turmeric, cumin, coriander, ginger, olive oil, and 1 of the garlic cloves in a bowl and stir well. Add the tuna, coating all the pieces with the mix. Cover and leave in the refrigerator to marinate for at least 1 hour, preferably overnight.

Mix the yogurt with the remaining garlic clove and the lemon zest and season with salt and pepper. Heat a griddle pan over a high heat and brush with a little vegetable oil. Sear the tuna pieces in batches for 1 minute on 1 side and 30 seconds on the other. Remove from the pan and serve with bamboo skewers for dipping into the yogurt sauce.

For seared tuna with wasabi mayonnaise, rub 13 oz fresh tuna steak, cut into chunks, with a little vegetable oil. Season with salt and a little ground Sichuan pepper, then sear in a hot griddle pan as above. Mix together 5 tablespoons mayonnaise with 1 tablespoon wasabi paste and 1 teaspoon lime juice. Serve with the seared tuna.

herring & dilled-cucumber skewers

Makes **15**
Preparation time **15 minutes**,
   plus chilling

15 canned or bottled **pickled
   herring fillets (matjes)**,
   drained, or 15 **roll-mop
   herrings**

Dilled cucumber
1 large **cucumber**
¾ cup **white wine vinegar**
2 teaspoons **superfine sugar**
3 tablespoons finely chopped
   dill weed
salt and **pepper**
**Pink beet & sour cream
   dipping sauce**, to serve
   (optional—see right)

Cut the cucumber into long, thin slices using a
vegetable peeler and put them in a shallow, nonmetallic bowl. Mix the vinegar with the sugar, stir in the
dill weed and pour over the cucumber. Season well with
salt and pepper, cover, and allow to pickle in the
refrigerator for 3–4 hours.

Thread a herring fillet or roll-mop herring onto a
wooden or bamboo skewer with some of the cucumber
slices. Repeat with the remaining herring and cucumber
to give you 15 skewers. Serve at room temperature with
the Pink Beet & Sour Cream Dipping Sauce (see
below), if desired.

For pink beet & sour cream dipping sauce,
to serve as an accompaniment, finely grate 2 oz
cooked, peeled beet in a food processor. Add
6 tablespoons sour cream and 6 tablespoons
mayonnaise and blend until fairly smooth and pink,
then chill until ready to use.

cajun calamari with avocado dip

Serves **4**
Preparation time **7 minutes**
Cooking time **8 minutes**

1¼ cups **all-purpose flour**
1 heaping tablespoon **Cajun seasoning**
4 large **squid**, cleaned (see page 12) and cut into rings, tentacles discarded
vegetable oil, for pan-frying
salt and **pepper**

Avocado dip

2 ripe **avocados**, peeled and pitted
1 small **red onion**, finely chopped
1 **red chili**, seeded and finely chopped
2 tablespoons **heavy cream**
juice of **1 lime**

Put the avocados in a food processor and blend until smooth (or simply mash with a fork). Stir in the onion, chili, and cream and season with the lime juice, salt, and pepper. Set aside while you prepare and cook the calamari.

Put the flour and Cajun seasoning in a large freezer bag along with a little salt and pepper. Mix well. Add the squid to the bag and shake well to coat all the squid in the flour mixture.

Heat ½ inch oil in a skillet over a high heat. Shake off the excess flour and fry the squid quickly in small batches for 1–2 minutes. Remove from the pan and drain on paper towels. Keep warm while you cook the remainder, then serve immediately with the avocado dip.

For breaded lime shrimp with chili mayonnaise, take 20 large raw shrimp, peeled but tails left on. Dust with all-purpose flour, then dip in beaten egg and finally roll in panko bread crumbs (Japanese bread crumbs) or dried white bread crumbs if panko are unavailable. Pan-fry in vegetable oil until golden, then squeeze over the juice of 1 lime. Mix 1 seeded and finely chopped red chili with ½ cup mayonnaise and serve with the lime shrimp.

crispy smelt & french fry cones

Makes **12** cones
Preparation time **20 minutes**
Cooking time **10 minutes**

8 oz **potatoes**, peeled and cut
 into long, thin French fries
sunflower oil, for deep-frying
4 tablespoons **all-purpose
 flour**
13 oz **smelt**
salt and **pepper**
malt vinegar, to serve

Line a large sheet of newspaper with waxed paper, cut the double layer into 12 squares, and twist each into a small cone.

Rinse the fries in cold water and dry thoroughly on paper towels. Pour the oil into a deep-fat fryer or large saucepan to a depth of at least 3 inches and heat to 350–375°F, or until a cube of bread browns in 30 seconds. Deep-fry the French fries for 4–5 minutes, then drain on paper towels and deep-fry them again for 1–2 minutes until crisp and golden. Drain the fries and keep them warm.

Put the flour on a large plate and season well with salt and pepper. Toss the smelt in the flour and fry in batches for 1–2 minutes, or until crisp and golden. Drain on paper towels.

Toss the smelt with the fries, season with salt, and pile into the paper cones. Serve the malt vinegar on the side.

For smelt with Indian spiced sweet potato wedges, peel 2 large sweet potatoes and cut into wedges. Place in a bowl with 2 tablespoons vegetable oil, 1 teaspoon ground cumin, 1 teaspoon ground coriander, and 1 teaspoon lightly crushed fennel seeds and toss together. Spread on a nonstick baking sheet and roast in a preheated oven, 400° F, for 30 minutes until tender in the center and crispy on the outside. Meanwhile, cook the smelt as above, then serve tossed with the potato wedges.

corn fritters with john dory

Serves **4**
Preparation time **10 minutes**
Cooking time **20 minutes**

2 tablespoons **olive oil**
2 **John Dory**, filleted, pin-
  boned, and cut into bite-size
  pieces
salt and **pepper**

Fritters
¾ cup **self-rising flour**
½ teaspoon **paprika**
1 **egg**
3 tablespoons **milk**
2 **corn ears**, kernels removed
1 **red bell pepper**, cored,
  seeded, and finely diced
2 tablespoons **vegetable oil**

To serve (optional)
6 tablespoons **sour cream**
a few **cilantro leaves**

Mix together the flour, paprika, egg, and milk to make a thick, smooth batter. Fold in the corn and red pepper and season with salt and pepper.

Heat the vegetable oil in a skillet over a medium heat. Drop in heaping teaspoonfuls of the fritter mixture and fry until golden and bubbles start to appear on the surface. Turn over and cook on the other side until brown. Keep warm while cooking the fish. (Alternatively, the fritters can also be made the day before and heated in the oven before serving.)

Heat a skillet over a high heat and add the olive oil. Season the fish and fry for 2 minutes until the skin is golden and crispy, then turn over and cook for 30 seconds more. Place a piece of fish on each fritter, topped with a spoonful of sour cream and garnished with a cilantro leaf, if desired.

For corn & pepper spoons with John Dory, mix together 1 cup canned, drained corn and 1 cored, seeded, and finely chopped red bell pepper. Add 1 teaspoon finely chopped red chili, 1 tablespoon chopped cilantro, and 1 tablespoon olive oil. Season with salt and pepper. Fry the John Dory as above. Place a little of the corn mixture in a silver dessert spoon and top with a piece of the fish and a squeeze of lime. Garnish with a cilantro sprig.

prosciutto & scallop kebabs

Makes **20**
Preparation time **20 minutes**,
  plus marinating
Cooking time **2–4 minutes**

2 **garlic cloves**, crushed
1 **dried red chili**, crushed
4 tablespoons **olive oil**
juice of ½ **orange**
1 teaspoon **dried oregano**
20 cleaned **sea scallops**,
  corals removed (optional)
10 thin slices of **prosciutto**,
  each cut into 2 strips
20 **basil leaves**
20 **sun-blushed tomato**
  halves
salt

Put the garlic, chili, oil, orange juice, and oregano in a small bowl, mix well, and season with salt.

Arrange the scallops in a single layer in a shallow bowl and pour over the garlic and chili mixture. Cover and leave in the refrigerator to marinate for 15–20 minutes.

Wrap a strip of prosciutto around each scallop and secure with a metal skewer or presoaked bamboo skewer. Add a basil leaf and a sun-blushed tomato half to each skewer.

Position the skewers about 2½ inches away from a broiler preheated to high and cook for 1–2 minutes on each side, or until the scallops have just cooked through. (Do not overcook or the scallops will become tough.) Remove from the broiler and serve immediately.

For citrus dressing, to serve as an accompaniment, place the juice of ½ orange and ½ grapefruit in a small saucepan. Bring to a boil and reduce until thick and syrupy. Pour into a bowl and beat in 3 tablespoons olive oil. Season with salt and pepper and add a little honey if the dressing is too sharp.

smoked salmon & cucumber sushi

Serves **4**

Preparation time **15 minutes**,
   plus cooling

Cooking time **15 minutes**

1½ cups **sushi rice**

2 tablespoons **rice vinegar**

1 tablespoon **superfine sugar**

2 **nori sheets**

1 teaspoon **wasabi paste**

2 long strips of **cucumber**, the
   length of the nori and about
   ½ inch thick

4 oz **smoked salmon**

2 tablespoons **pickled ginger**

4 tablespoons **soy sauce**

Cook the sushi rice according to the instructions on the package.

Mix together the vinegar and sugar and stir until the sugar dissolves. Once the rice is cooked and when it is still warm, mix in enough of the vinegar and sugar mixture to coat the rice grains, but do not allow the rice to become wet. Tip the rice onto a tray to cool quickly.

Take 1 nori sheet and place it on a bamboo mat with the longest side in line with your body and the ridged surface facing upward. With damp hands, cover three-quarters of the nori sheet with a thin layer of rice, leaving a band of nori at the top without rice.

Spread a little wasabi paste with your finger on top of the rice in a thin line, at the edge nearest to you. Then place a cucumber strip and some smoked salmon on top.

Use the bamboo mat to start rolling the nori up, tucking in the cucumber and salmon as you go. Once you have rolled up the majority of the nori, wet your finger and dampen the plain edge of nori. Finish rolling up the nori and the wet edge will stick the roll together. Repeat with the other nori sheet. Then, using a sharp knife, cut the rolls into 8 even pieces.

Mix the remaining wasabi with the pickled ginger and soy sauce and serve alongside the nori rolls.

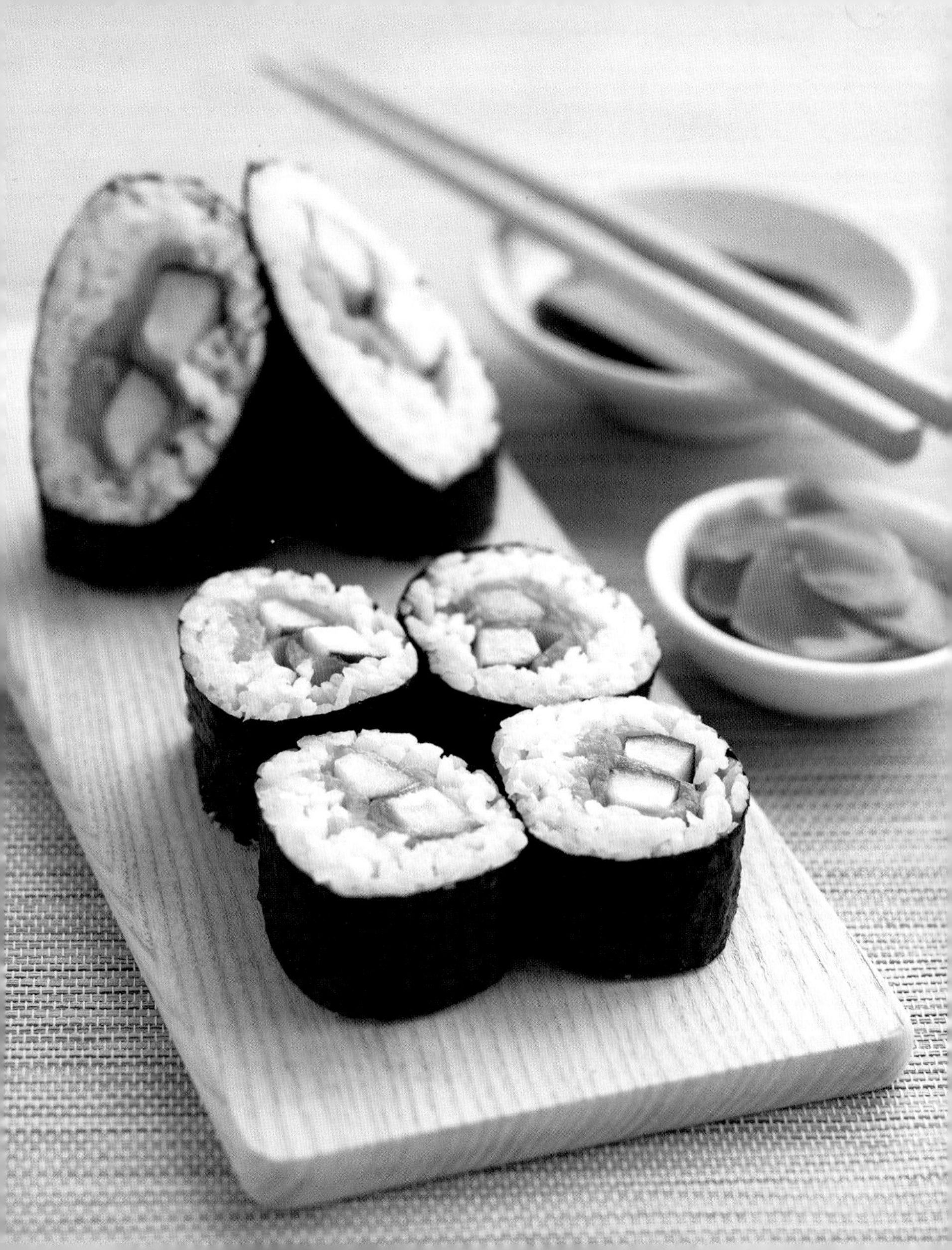

chili crab on mini noodle nests

Makes **20**
Preparation time **10 minutes**
Cooking time **11–15 minutes**

4 oz **fresh fine egg noodles**
1 tablespoon **sunflower oil**,
    plus extra for greasing
2 **scallions**, finely sliced
2 **garlic cloves**, finely chopped
1 teaspoon peeled and finely
    diced **fresh ginger root**
1 **red chili**, seeded and finely
    diced
7 oz **fresh white crabmeat**
2 tablespoons **sweet chili
    sauce**
4 tablespoons finely chopped
    cilantro

Grease 20 nonstick mini tartlet cups lightly with oil.
Divide the noodles into 20 portions and press each
portion into a tartlet cup to form a tartlet shape, making
sure the base is covered. Lightly brush with more oil
and put in a preheated oven, 350°F, for 8–10 minutes,
or until crisp and firm. Remove from the cups and allow
to cool on a cooling rack.

Heat the 1 tablespoon oil in a large, nonstick wok or
skillet and add the scallions, garlic, ginger, and chili and
stir-fry for 2–3 minutes. Add the crabmeat and stir-fry
for an additional 1–2 minutes, then remove from the
heat, stir in the sweet chili sauce and cilantro, and toss
to mix well.

Place a heaping teaspoonful of the chili crab mixture
into each cooled noodle nest and serve immediately.

For chili crab linguine, cook 10 oz linguine according
to the instructions on the package. Drain and set
aside. Heat 2 tablespoons olive oil in a large skillet
and fry 1 finely chopped large red chili for 2 minutes.
Stir in 4 finely sliced scallions, 12 oz fresh white
crabmeat, the juice of 1 lime, and 2 tablespoons
roughly chopped cilantro leaves and warm through.
Add the linguine and toss all the ingredients together.
Dress the crab linguine with 2 tablespoons olive oil
and serve immediately.

sweet chili & ginger pollock

Serves **4**

Preparation time **15 minutes**

Cooking time **20 minutes**

1¼ cups **self-rising flour**

1 tablespoon **cornstarch**

2 tablespoons chopped
   cilantro

½ cup **sparkling water**

14 oz **pollock fillet**, pin-boned
   and cut into 3 x 1 inch strips

vegetable oil, for deep-frying

salt and **pepper**

1 **lime**, cut into wedges,
   to garnish

Sauce

3 tablespoons **sweet chili
   sauce**

1 tablespoon finely chopped
   pickled ginger, plus
   1 teaspoon of the juice

Mix the sauce ingredients together and set aside.

Place the flour, cornstarch, cilantro, and a good pinch of
salt and pepper in a large bowl. Using a fork, stir in the
sparkling water to make a batter of the consistency of
heavy cream. Do not overstir the batter: small lumps
of flour are fine. Pat the fish strips dry on paper towels
and dip into the batter.

Pour the oil into a deep-fat fryer or large saucepan
to a depth of at least 3 inches and heat to 350–375°F,
or until a cube of bread browns in 30 seconds. Cook
the fish in small batches until it is golden brown.
Drain on paper towels and keep warm while you cook
the remainder.

Serve the goujons with the sauce, garnished with the
lime wedges.

For homemade tartare sauce, to serve as an
alternative accompaniment, mix together ⅔ cup
mayonnaise, 1 tablespoon each gherkins, capers,
and shallot, all finely chopped, and 2 tablespoons
chopped parsley. Season with salt and pepper.

anchovy puff pastry straws

Serves **4**
Preparation time **10 minutes**
Cooking time **10 minutes**

2 sheets of **ready-rolled puff pastry**, thawed if frozen
2 oz **canned anchovy fillets**, drained and finely chopped
4 tablespoons finely grated **Parmesan cheese**
1 **egg**, lightly beaten
1 tablespoon **black sesame seeds**

Lay 1 sheet of the puff pastry on the work surface. Spread the anchovies over it and sprinkle with the Parmesan.

Brush the top of the other sheet of pastry with a little beaten egg. Place this on top of the anchovy and cheese mixture, egg wash-side down, to make a puff pastry sandwich. Roll over the puff pastry sandwich with a rolling pin to seal the 2 sheets together. It should be about the same thickness as 1 of the original sheets of pastry. Brush the top of the sandwich with a little beaten egg and sprinkle with a few black sesame seeds.

Cut the sandwich into 4 x ¾ inch strips and place on a nonstick baking sheet, leaving room between them to allow them to expand.

Place the straws in a preheated oven, 400°F, and bake for 10 minutes, or until risen and golden brown. Remove from the oven and cool on a cooling rack.

For anchovy & black olive phyllo pastry straws, take 1 sheet of phyllo pastry and brush it with a little melted butter. Place another sheet on top and brush with melted butter. Mix together 2 oz canned, drained anchovy fillets and ⅓ cup pitted black olives, chopped. Spread a little of this mixture at the edge of the phyllo pastry, then start to roll it up into a straw shape. Cut each straw in half. Brush the outside of the straws with more melted butter and bake in a preheated oven, 375°F, for 8–10 minutes, or until golden brown.

lobster & tarragon puffs

Makes **20**
Preparation time **20 minutes**
Cooking time **12–15 minutes**

7 oz **puff pastry**, thawed if
frozen
all-purpose flour, for dusting
2 **eggs**, lightly beaten, for
glazing
5 oz **cooked lobster tail
meat**, chopped into ½ inch
dice
4 tablespoons **mayonnaise**
1 teaspoon **American-style
mustard**
1 tablespoon cored, seeded,
and very finely diced **red bell
pepper**
2 tablespoons very finely
chopped **tarragon**
salt and **pepper**
tarragon sprigs, to garnish

Line a large baking sheet with nonstick parchment
paper. Roll the pastry out on a lightly floured surface
to ¼ inch thick. Stamp out 40 x 2½ inch rounds using
a cookie or pastry cutter. Put 20 of the rounds on the
baking sheet, spaced well apart, and brush with beaten
egg. Using a 1¼ inch cutter, stamp out circles from the
center of the remaining rounds. Discard the inner pastry
circles, leaving you with 20 pastry "rings." Put these
"rings" on the brushed pastry rounds and press gently
to seal. Brush again with the beaten egg, then bake in
a preheated oven, 400°F, for 12–15 minutes, or until
risen and golden. Remove from the oven and transfer
to a cooling rack to cool completely.

Meanwhile, put the lobster meat in a bowl and mix in
the mayonnaise, mustard, red pepper, and chopped
tarragon. Season well with salt and pepper. Using a
teaspoon, carefully spoon the mixture into the cold
puff shells. Garnish with tarragon sprigs and
serve immediately.

For shrimp wrapped in puff pastry blankets, roll
out 7 oz puff pastry until it is ⅛ inch thick. Take 15 large
raw jumbo shrimp and remove their heads and shells,
leaving the very end of the tails on. Cut the sheet of
puff pastry into 2 inch squares. Brush the edges with a
little beaten egg. Wrap each shrimp in a pastry square,
leaving the end of the tail exposed. Trim any excess
pastry. Brush the tops with beaten egg and sprinkle
with sesame seeds. Bake in a preheated oven, 350° F,
for 10–15 minutes until golden brown.

crayfish rolls with hoisin sauce

Serves **4**
Preparation time **25 minutes**

8 rice paper sheets
16 long **chives**
4 **iceberg lettuce leaves**,
  finely shredded
4 **scallions**, finely shredded
  into matchsticks
16 **mint leaves**, shredded
16 **cooked peeled crayfish
  tails**
3 tablespoons **hoisin sauce**

Fill a shallow bowl with hot water and soak the rice paper sheets for around 5 minutes until softened. Remove the sheets from the water and place on a clean, dry dish towel. Cut in half.

Blanch the chives in boiling water for 10 seconds, then cool under cold running water.

Take 1 half sheet of rice paper and fill with a little lettuce, scallions, mint, and a crayfish tail. Roll the rice paper sheet to enclose these ingredients, folding in the ends to enclose everything. Tie a chive around the center of the roll to seal it closed, then place on a tray covered with a clean, damp dish towel while you make the remaining rolls. Serve the crayfish rolls with the hoisin sauce for dipping.

For shrimp & bamboo shoot spring rolls, brush 1 sheet of phyllo pastry with a little melted butter. With the short side of the pastry in line with your body, place 1 raw peeled jumbo shrimp and a small pile of bamboo shoots in the center of the pastry at the edge. Roll the phyllo pastry sheet to enclose these ingredients, folding in the ends to enclose everything. Repeat with 15 more sheets of phyllo pastry, 15 more shrimp, and some bamboo shoots. Brush the spring rolls with melted butter and bake in a preheated oven, 350°F, for 10–15 minutes until golden brown. Serve with hoisin sauce for dipping.

soba, tobiko, & scallion spoons

Makes **20**
Preparation time **15 minutes**
Cooking time **5 minutes**

8 oz **dried soba noodles**
4 tablespoons **light soy sauce**
4 tablespoons **mirin** (rice wine)
1 teaspoon **toasted sesame oil**
¼ teaspoon **wasabi paste**
6 tablespoons **sunflower oil**
2 **scallions**, very finely sliced
1 oz **tobiko** (flying fish roe) or small salmon roe

Cook the noodles according to the instructions on the package until just tender. Drain, rinse in cold water, and drain again.

Beat the soy sauce with the mirin, sesame oil, wasabi paste, and sunflower oil in a bowl until well blended. Add the noodles and toss gently to coat evenly, then stir in the scallions and toss to mix well.

Divide the noodles into 20 bite-size portions and twirl each portion with a fork to make a neat nest. Carefully transfer to individual oriental soup spoons, then, using a teaspoon, top each nest with a little tobiko or salmon roe and serve immediately.

For soba noodle & crayfish salad, cook the noodles according to the instructions on the package, drain, and set aside. Mix together 2 tablespoons sweet chili sauce, the juice of 1 lime, and 2 tablespoons Thai fish sauce. Pour the sauce over the drained noodles and mix well. Add ¼ cup salted peanuts, 7 oz cooked peeled crayfish tails, and 4 sliced scallions, and serve garnished with a large handful of cilantro leaves.

rosemary scones & smoked trout

Serves **4**

Preparation time **30 minutes**

Cooking time **7–10 minutes**

2 cups **self-rising flour**, plus
extra for dusting

pinch of **salt**

½ teaspoon **baking powder**

¼ cup **butter**, diced

1 tablespoon finely chopped
rosemary

1 **egg**, lightly beaten

around ⅔ cup **buttermilk**

milk, for glazing

a few **dill sprigs**, to garnish
(optional)

Topping

½ cup **cream cheese**

1 tablespoon chopped **dill
weed**

1 tablespoon chopped **chives**

5 oz **smoked trout**

salt and **pepper**

Sift the flour, salt, and baking powder into a bowl and blend in the butter with your fingertips until the mixture resembles bread crumbs. Stir in the rosemary, egg, and enough buttermilk to give a soft but not sticky dough. Don't overwork the mixture.

Roll the dough out on a lightly floured surface to a thickness of ¾ inch. Using a 1¼ inch cookie or pastry cutter, cut out 16 rounds. Place them on a nonstick baking sheet and brush the tops with a little milk. Place them in a preheated oven, 375°F, for 7–10 minutes, or until golden brown and risen, then transfer to a cooling rack to cool.

Mix together the cream cheese, dill weed, and chives and season with salt and pepper.

Cut the top off each scone to give a flat surface, then spread a little of the cream cheese mixture on top. Place a little smoked trout on the cream cheese mixture and garnish with a dill sprig, if desired.

For smoked salmon pâté, to serve as an alternative topping for the scones, blend 8 oz smoked salmon with 2 tablespoons cream and 6 tablespoons cream cheese in a food processor. Stir in 2 tablespoons chopped dill weed and season with salt and pepper.

potted shrimp with herby pitas

Serves **4**

Preparation time **10 minutes**, plus chilling

Cooking time **15 minutes**

1 tablespoon **olive oil**

1 small **red onion**, finely chopped

1 **green chilli**, seeded and finely chopped

1 cup **butter**

7 oz **cooked peeled brown shrimp**

grated zest of 1 **lime**, and about 1 teaspoon juice

salt and **pepper**

Herby pitas

¼ cup **butter**, softened

1 **garlic clove**, crushed

1 tablespoon finely chopped **cilantro**

1 tablespoon finely chopped **parsley**

4 white or whole-wheat **pita breads**

Heat the oil in a skillet over a medium heat. Add the onion and chili and fry until the onion is soft and translucent. Remove from the heat, add the butter and let it melt. Finally, add the shrimp and lime zest. Season the shrimp with a squeeze of lime juice to taste and some salt and pepper.

Spoon the mixture into individual ramekins or a large serving ramekin. Cover and place in the refrigerator for at least 2 hours, or until the butter has set. (This can easily be done the day before.) Remove from the refrigerator 20 minutes before serving.

Place the softened butter in a small bowl. Mix in the garlic, cilantro, and parsley and season to taste with salt and pepper. Make a cut in each pita bread to open up the pocket inside and spread with 1 teaspoon of the butter mixture.

Wrap the pita breads in foil and place in a preheated oven, 350°F, for 8−10 minutes, or until warmed through and the butter has melted. Serve with the potted shrimp.

For traditional potted shrimp, melt 1 cup butter in a saucepan. Remove from the heat and stir in a pinch each of ground mace, nutmeg, and paprika. Add 7 oz cooked peeled brown shrimp, season with salt and pepper, and pour into individual ramekins, then chill. Serve with toasted sourdough.

soups & stews

onion & bean soup with shrimp

Serves **4**
Preparation time **25 minutes**
Cooking time **20 minutes**

2 tablespoons **olive oil**
10 **scallions**, roughly
  chopped, plus extra, finely
  chopped to garnish
1 **garlic clove**, roughly
  chopped
a few **thyme leaves**
2 x 13 oz cans **lima beans**,
  drained and rinsed
3 cups **chicken stock** or
  Basic Fish Stock (see
  page 15)
6 tablespoons **heavy cream**
20 **raw peeled jumbo
  shrimp**, deveined
salt and **pepper**
2 tablespoons finely chopped
  chives, to garnish

Heat 1 tablespoon of the oil in a saucepan. Add the roughly chopped scallions, garlic, and thyme leaves and fry over a gentle heat until soft. Add the beans, stock, and cream. Bring the soup to a boil, then reduce the heat and simmer for 5 minutes.

Transfer the soup to a blender or food processor and blend until smooth. If it is a little thick, add a little more cream or stock. Season the soup with salt and pepper.

Place a skillet over a high heat and add the remaining oil. Season the shrimp with salt and pepper, then fry them in the pan for 4 minutes, or until they turn pink.

Stack the shrimp in the center of 4 bowls and pour the soup around them. Garnish the dish with a few chopped scallions and the chives.

For scallops with white bean puree, heat a little olive oil in a pan. Gently fry 1 finely chopped onion and 1 crushed garlic clove. Add 2 x 13 oz cans lima beans, drained and rinsed, and 3 tablespoons heavy cream to the pan to warm through. Transfer the mixture to a blender or food processor and blend to form a rough or smooth puree, depending on taste. A little more cream may be needed. Season to taste. Heat 1 tablespoon olive oil in a skillet over a very high heat. Season 12 cleaned scallops with a little salt, pepper, and mild curry powder, then fry for 1 minute on each side. Serve on top of the bean puree with an arugula salad dressed with a little lemon juice and olive oil.

spiced angler fish & chickpea stew

Serves **4**

Preparation time **10 minutes**

Cooking time **20 minutes**

2 tablespoons **vegetable oil**

1 **onion**, finely chopped

2 **garlic cloves**, crushed

¼ teaspoon **chili powder**

1 tablespoon **curry powder**

¼ teaspoon **turmeric**

1 tablespoon **tomato paste**

2 x 13 oz cans **tomatoes**

6 tablespoons **chicken stock**
    or **Basic Fish Stock** (see
    page 15)

1½ lb **angler fish tail**, cut into
    large chunks

13 oz can **chickpeas**, drained

1 tablespoon **Homemade
    Mango Chutney** (see page
    122)

4 tablespoons **plain yogurt**

large handful of **cilantro
    leaves**

salt and **pepper**

Heat the oil in a large saucepan. Add the onion and fry gently until soft but not browned. Add the garlic, chili powder, curry powder, and turmeric to the pan and fry for 2 minutes until the spices become fragrant. Add the tomato paste, tomatoes, and stock and bring to a boil, then reduce the heat and simmer for 10 minutes. If the stew becomes too dry, add a little more stock.

Stir in the angler fish and chickpeas and bring to a boil, then reduce the heat and simmer for 5 minutes, or until the angler fish is cooked. Finally, stir in the mango chutney and season to taste with a little salt and pepper. Serve in bowls, topped with a spoonful of yogurt and some cilantro leaves.

For cumin- & fennel-spiced chapatis, to serve as an accompaniment, sift together 1 cup all-purpose flour and ½ cup whole-wheat flour, discarding any bits of bran left in the sifter. Gently toast 1 tablespoon each cumin seeds and fennel seeds in a pan, then crush them using a mortar and pestle. Add the crushed spices to the flour with a good pinch of salt. Mix in enough water to give you a smooth dough. Wrap the dough in plastic wrap and allow to rest for 1 hour. Heat a skillet over a high heat. Divide the dough into 8 pieces and form into balls. Roll 1 of the balls into a thin, flat disk. Place in the pan for 40 seconds, flipping it a few times. Repeat with the rest of the dough. Keep the chapatis warm in a clean dish towel.

crab bisque with garlic croutons

Serves **4**
Preparation time **12 minutes**
Cooking time **40 minutes**

shells of 2 large **crabs**
4 tablespoons **olive oil**
1 **onion**, chopped
2 **carrots**, chopped
2 **celery sticks**, chopped
1 **bay leaf**
2 tablespoons **Cognac**
4 ripe **tomatoes**, roughly
  chopped
2 teaspoons **tomato paste**
4 cups **Basic Fish Stock** (see
  page 15)
2 **garlic cloves**, finely chopped
4 thick slices of **white bread**,
  crusts removed and cut into
  ½ inch cubes
6 tablespoons **heavy cream**
pinch of **cayenne pepper**
salt and **pepper**

Break up the crab shells using the back of a large knife and a mallet.

Heat 2 tablespoons of the oil in a large saucepan. Add the onion, carrots, celery, and bay leaf and fry until soft but not browned. Add the broken shells and fry for 2–3 minutes, then add the Cognac, tomatoes, and tomato paste.

Pour in the stock and bring to a boil, then reduce the heat and simmer for 30 minutes.

Heat the remaining oil in a skillet and add the garlic. Fry for 1 minute to flavor the oil, then remove and discard the garlic. Add the bread cubes to the garlic oil and fry until golden brown.

Remove the claw shell from the pan. Place the rest of the shells and liquid in a blender or food processor in batches and blend until the shells are in pieces of about ½ inch. Pass the liquid and shells through a fine sieve lined with a piece of cheesecloth.

Pour the liquid back into a clean saucepan and bring to a boil, then add the cream and cayenne. If the flavor needs intensifying, simmer the soup to reduce it. Season with salt and pepper and serve in bowls topped with the garlic croutons.

smoked haddock chowder

Serves **4**

Preparation time **15 minutes**

Cooking time **30 minutes**

4 large, round **white bread rolls**

1 **egg**, lightly beaten

¼ cup **butter**

8 **scallions** chopped

1 **garlic clove**, crushed

2 large, **waxy potatoes**, peeled and cut into cubes

1½ cups **milk**

¾ cup **heavy cream**

¾ cup **Basic Fish Stock** (see page 15)

1 cup **canned corn**, drained

1 lb **smoked haddock**, skinned and cut into large chunks

1 tablespoon **olive oil**

8 **bacon** slices

2 tablespoons chopped **parsley**

salt and **pepper**

Cut the tops off the bread rolls and pull out the soft center, leaving a bowl shape and a lid. Place on a baking sheet in a preheated oven, 325°F, and bake for 25 minutes until they have dried out and become crispy. Brush the inside of the bread rolls with the egg. Place the rolls back in the oven for an additional 5 minutes to dry out once again. Remove from the oven and set aside.

Heat the butter in a large saucepan. Add the scallions and fry until soft. Add the garlic and potatoes and fry for a minute more. Pour in the milk, cream, and stock and bring the soup to a boil, then reduce the heat and simmer for 10 minutes, or until the potatoes are almost cooked.

Add the corn and smoked haddock to the pan and simmer for an additional 5 minutes until the fish has cooked. Season with salt and pepper.

Heat the oil in a skillet and fry the bacon until crispy. When ready to serve, place the bread bowls in shallow bowls. Pour the soup into the bread bowls, then top with the bacon and a sprinkling of parsley.

For clam chowder, follow the recipe above but replace the smoked haddock with 2 lb cleaned clams (see page 12). Heat a saucepan over a high heat and add 6 tablespoons white wine. Tip in the clams, cover, and steam until they open, discarding any that don't. Strain the clams and pick about half of the clams out of their shells. Add these to the soup with the corn, along with the clams that are still in their shells. Serve as above.

vegetable broth & sea bass

Serves **4**
Preparation time **5 minutes**
Cooking time **7–8 minutes**

3 cups good-quality **chicken**
  or **vegetable stock**
2 tablespoons **olive oil**
4 **sea bass fillets**, about
  7 oz each, skin on, pin-boned
1 **fennel bulb**, cut into
  8, herby tops reserved
12 **fine asparagus spears**
1 cup **frozen peas**, thawed
1 cup **fava beans**
small handful of **mint leaves**,
  torn
small handful of **basil leaves**,
  torn
salt and **pepper**

Bring the stock to a boil in a saucepan.

Heat the oil in a skillet. Season the sea bass with salt and pepper and place, skin-side down, in the pan. Cook for 3–4 minutes until the skin is crispy, then turn the fish over and cook for 1 minute on the other side.

Meanwhile, place the fennel in the stock and simmer for 3 minutes, or until it is just starting to become tender. Add the asparagus, peas, and fava beans to the pan and cook for an additional 1–2 minutes. Season the broth with salt and pepper.

Divide the vegetable broth between 4 bowls and sprinkle with a few torn mint and basil leaves. Top the dish with the pan-fried sea bass and reserved herby fennel tops and serve.

For Thai broth with shrimp, peel and devein 1 lb raw jumbo shrimp, reserving the shells and heads. Heat 3 cups Basic Fish Stock (see page 15) or chicken stock in a saucepan. Add the shrimp shells and heads, 2 roughly chopped lemon grass stalks, a 2 inch piece of fresh ginger root, 1 dried red chili, and 2 kaffir lime leaves. Allow the stock to infuse off the heat for 30 minutes. Strain the stock and return it to a clean saucepan. Add the shrimp and poach for 3–4 minutes until cooked. Add 4 oz sugar snap peas at the last minute.

tomato stew with clams & chorizo

Serves **4**
Preparation time **15 minutes**
Cooking time **20–25 minutes**

10 oz **chorizo sausage**, cut
  into chunks
1 teaspoon **coriander seeds**,
  crushed
1 tablespoon **fennel seeds**,
  crushed
1 **onion**, finely chopped
1 **red chili**, seeded and finely
  chopped
2 **garlic cloves**, crushed
3 tablespoons **white wine**
13 oz can **chopped tomatoes**
¾ cup **Basic Fish Stock** (see
  page 15)
1 lb **clams**, cleaned (see
  page 12)
a few **basil leaves**, to garnish

Heat a large saucepan over a high heat. Add the
chorizo and fry until the natural oil has been released
and the chorizo is starting to brown. Remove the chorizo
from the pan, leaving behind its oil, and set aside.

Fry the coriander and fennel seeds in the chorizo oil
for 1 minute, then add the onion and chili and fry until
the onion has softened but not browned. Add the garlic
and fry for a minute more. Pour in the wine and allow
to bubble until just 1 tablespoon of liquid is left. Add
the tomatoes and stock, bring the stew to a boil, and
return the chorizo to the pan. Tip in the clams, then
cover and cook until the clams have opened,
discarding any that don't.

Divide the stew between 4 bowls, garnish with a few
basil leaves, and serve with crusty bread.

For spicy bean stew with pan-fried John Dory,
follow the recipe above but omit the clams and chorizo
and add 13 oz can navy beans and 13 oz can kidney
beans, drained. Pan-fry the fillets of 2 John Dory and
serve with the bean stew.

cuttlefish stew

Serves **4**

Preparation time **15 minutes**

Cooking time **1 hour 10 minutes**

2 tablespoons **olive oil**

1 **onion**, finely chopped

1 **fennel bulb**, finely chopped

2 **garlic cloves**, crushed

1 tablespoon **smoked paprika**

1 tablespoon **paprika**

2 tablespoons **tomato paste**

2 x 13 oz cans **chopped tomatoes**

⅔ cup **red wine**

2 lb **cuttlefish**, cleaned and cut into strips

13 oz can **lima beans**, drained

1 teaspoon **superfine sugar** (optional)

2 tablespoons finely chopped **parsley**

Heat the oil in a large saucepan. Add the onion and fennel and fry until the onion is soft but not browned. Add the garlic and paprika and fry for a minute more. Add the tomato paste, tomatoes, wine, and cuttlefish. Bring the stew to a boil, then reduce the heat, cover, and simmer for 1 hour, or until the cuttlefish is tender. If the dish becomes a little dry, add some water or stock.

Add the lima beans and warm through. Taste and add the sugar if necessary. Finally, add the parsley and serve with warm crusty bread or Lemon and Parsley Mashed Potatoes (see below).

For lemon & parsley mashed potatoes, to serve as an accompaniment, peel 4 floury potatoes, cut into pieces and boil in lightly salted water until tender. Drain and mash the potatoes. Beat in ½ cup butter and enough cream to make a really creamy mash. Grate in the zest of 1 lemon and 2 tablespoons finely chopped parsley. Season to taste with salt and pepper.

shrimp & pork wonton soup

Serves **4**

Preparation time **25 minutes**

Cooking time **5–6 minutes**

4 oz **ground pork**

5 oz **raw peeled shrimp**

4 **scallions**, finely chopped

1 **garlic clove**

½ inch piece of **fresh ginger root**, peeled and chopped

1 tablespoon **oyster sauce**

20 **wonton wrappers**

3 cups **chicken stock**

1 head of **Chinese greens**, shredded

1–2 tablespoons **Thai fish sauce**

To serve

leaves from a small bunch of **cilantro**

1 tablespoon **sesame seeds**

1 **lime**, cut into wedges (optional)

Place the pork, shrimp, 2 of the scallions, the garlic, ginger, and oyster sauce in a food processor and blend to a paste.

Take 1 of the wonton wrappers and place 1 teaspoon of the shrimp and pork mixture in the center. Dampen the edges of the wrapper with a little water and bring them up around the filling, enclosing it completely in a little bundle. Repeat with the remainder of the wrappers and shrimp and pork mixture.

Bring the stock to a boil in a large saucepan, then reduce the heat, add the wontons, and simmer for 4–5 minutes. Remove 1 of the wontons and check that it has become firm, which will indicate that it is cooked.

Add the greens to the pan and cook for 1 minute. Season the stock with the fish sauce.

Divide the soup between 4 bowls and serve with a few cilantro leaves, a sprinkling of sesame seeds, and a lime wedge.

For sesame wontons with soy dipping sauce, make the wontons as per the recipe above and steam them in a bamboo steamer for 5 minutes. Remove the wontons from the steamer and sprinkle over 2 tablespoons sesame seeds. Make a dipping sauce by mixing together 3 tablespoons light soy sauce, 2 teaspoons grated fresh ginger root, 1 finely sliced red chili, and 1 tablespoon Thai fish sauce.

thai coconut soup

Serves **4**

Preparation time **20 minutes**

Cooking time **15 minutes**

7 oz **dried rice noodles**

3 tablespoons **vegetable oil**

2 **shallots**, very finely chopped

1 **green chili**, seeded and very finely chopped

2 **lemon grass stalks**, bottom two-thirds only, very finely chopped

2 inch piece of **fresh ginger root**, peeled and grated

1¾ cups **coconut milk**

1¼ cups **chicken stock**

2 tablespoons **Thai fish sauce**

juice of 1½ **limes**

1 teaspoon **brown sugar**

13 oz **angler fish tail**, cut into large chunks

8 oz **mussels**, scrubbed and debearded (see page 12)

4 **red mullet fillets**, pin-boned

salt and **pepper**

Place the noodles in a heatproof bowl and cover with boiling water. Leave for 5 minutes, then drain.

Heat 2 tablespoons of the oil in a large saucepan. Add the shallots, chili, lemon grass, and ginger and fry over a gentle heat until the shallot has softened. Add the coconut milk and stock and bring to a boil, then reduce the heat and simmer for 5 minutes to infuse the flavors. Season the soup by adding the fish sauce, the juice of 1 lime, and the sugar. Adjust quantities to taste.

Add the drained noodles and the angler fish to the soup and cook for 2 minutes. Discard any mussels that don't shut when tapped, then add to the soup. Cook until they open and the angler fish is firm.

Meanwhile, heat the remaining oil in a skillet. Season the mullet with salt and pepper and fry, skin-side down, for 3 minutes, or until the skin becomes crispy. Turn the fish over and cook for a minute more. Squeeze the remaining lime juice over the fish.

Divide the soup between 4 bowls, removing any mussels that have not opened, and top with the mullet.

For mussels in saffron broth, sweat a finely chopped onion and 2 finely chopped garlic cloves in a little oil in a saucepan. Add a large glass of white wine, a pinch of saffron threads, and 3 lb scrubbed and debearded mussels to the pan (first discarding any that don't shut when tapped), cover, and cook until the mussels open (discarding any that don't), removing the lid and stirring once or twice during the cooking process. Add ¾ cup heavy cream and a large handful of chopped parsley, stir well, and season.

salads & appetizers

seared salmon with avocado salad

Serves **4**
Preparation time **15 minutes**
Cooking time **10–12 minutes**

2 tablespoons **olive oil**
4 pieces of **salmon fillet**,
    about 7 oz each, skin on and
    pin-boned
1 large **orange**
2 tablespoons **extra virgin
    olive oil**
salt and **pepper**

Avocado salad
2 ripe **avocados**, peeled and
    cut into ½ inch dice
1 **red chili**, deseeded and
    finely chopped
juice of **1 lime**
1 tablespoon roughly chopped
    cilantro
1 tablespoon **olive oil**

Heat a small skillet over a high heat. When the pan is hot, add the olive oil. Season the salmon with salt and pepper and place it, skin-side down, in the pan. Cook for 4 minutes, then turn the fish over and cook for an additional 2 minutes.

Heat another small skillet on the burner. Cut the orange in half and place the orange halves, cut-side down, in the pan. Sear the orange halves until they start to blacken. Remove the oranges from the pan and squeeze the juice into the skillet. Bring the juice to a boil and reduce it until you have around 1 tablespoon left. Beat in the extra virgin olive oil and season with salt and pepper.

Place the avocados in a mixing bowl, add the remaining ingredients, and season with salt and pepper.

Spoon the avocado salad into the center of each plate. Place a piece of salmon on top and drizzle with the burnt orange vinaigrette.

For salmon with orange couscous, pan-fry 4 salmon steaks as above. Bring 1¾ cups freshly squeezed orange juice to a boil in a saucepan with 2 tablespoons raisins. Place 1¾ cups couscous in a heatproof bowl and pour over the orange juice. Cover the bowl with plastic wrap and allow the couscous to steam for 5 minutes before fluffing the grains up with a fork. Add 1 tablespoon olive oil, a large handful of chopped cilantro and 2 tablespoons pine nuts. Serve with sour cream and the warm salmon.

flounder with fennel salad

Serves **4**
Preparation time **20 minutes**
Cooking time **5–10 minutes**

Salad
1 **fennel bulb**, finely sliced
1⅓ cups **frozen peas**, thawed
1¼ cups **fava beans**
5 **radishes**, finely sliced
2 cups **watercress**

Dressing
1 tablespoon **wholegrain mustard**
1 teaspoon **honey**
1 tablespoon **white wine vinegar**
3 tablespoons **olive oil**
salt and **pepper**

Fish
2 tablespoons **olive oil**
4 **flounder fillets**, skin on and pin-boned
2 tablespoons **all-purpose flour**, seasoned wth salt and pepper
1 **lemon**

Place the fennel in a bowl along with the peas, fava beans, radishes, and watercress.

Make the dressing by mixing together the mustard, honey, vinegar, and oil. Season to taste with salt and pepper. Add enough of the dressing to the salad to coat all the ingredients. Set aside while you cook the flounder.

Heat a little of the oil in a very hot skillet and dust the flounder fillets with the seasoned flour. Place the fish, skin-side down, in the pan. Cook for 3 minutes on the skin side, then carefully turn the fish over and cook for an additional 2 minutes. (Depending on the size of your pan, you may need to cook the fish in 2 batches.) Once the fish is cooked, squeeze a little lemon juice over the fish and serve with the fennel salad.

For hot honey & mustard salmon, mix together 1 heaping tablespoon wholegrain mustard and 2 tablespoons honey. Pour over 4 skinless salmon fillets and place in a preheated oven, 350°F, for about 8–10 minutes or until cooked. Serve with buttered new potatoes.

mackerel with baked beets

Serves **4**
Preparation time **15 minutes**
Cooking time **1 hour**
  5 minutes

4 small **mackerel**, filleted
1 tablespoon **olive oil**
salt and **pepper**

Beet
2 large **raw beets**
2 **garlic cloves**, sliced
4 **thyme sprigs**
2 tablespoons **olive oil**, plus
  extra for drizzling

**Horseradish Cream
  (optional)**
⅔ cup **sour cream**
2 tablespoons **mayonnaise**
2 tablespoons finely chopped
  chives
1–2 tablespoons **creamed
  horseradish**

Wash the beets well. Wrap the beets in a foil parcel with the garlic, thyme, salt and pepper to taste, and oil. Place in a preheated oven, 350°F, for around 1 hour until the beet is cooked and a knife can easily be inserted into the center. Once cool enough to handle, peel the beets. Cut into bite-size pieces, drizzle with a little oil, and season with salt and pepper. Set aside.

Mix together all the horseradish cream ingredients, if using, and season with salt and pepper.

Place the fish on a nonstick baking sheet, skin-side up. Brush the skin with the oil and season with salt and pepper. Cook under a preheated broiler on this side until the skin is crispy, about 3 minutes, then carefully turn over and cook for an additional 2 minutes on the other side.

Serve the mackerel with the roasted beet and horseradish cream, if using.

For smoked mackerel pâté, place 10 oz skinless smoked mackerel in a food processor with 3 tablespoons sour cream and 2 tablespoons horseradish sauce. Blend until smooth, then fold in lemon juice to taste and season with salt and pepper. Serve with toast.

deviled oysters

Serves **4**

Preparation time **25 minutes**

Cooking time **15 minutes**

12 **oysters**

1 teaspoon **mustard seeds**

⅓ cup **butter**

2 **shallots**, finely chopped

½ **celery stick**, finely chopped

1 **garlic clove**, crushed

1 tablespoon **white wine vinegar**

1 teaspoon **Tabasco sauce**

1 tablespoon chopped **chives**

1 tablespoon chopped **flat leaf parsley**

plenty of **sea salt** and **pepper**

Hold an oyster, wrapped in a heavyweight cloth, with the rounded shell underneath. Push a strong knife, preferably an oyster knife, into the small gap at the hinged end. Twist the knife to sever the muscle and separate the shells.

Discard the top shell. Run the blade of the knife under the oyster to loosen it, holding the shell steady to prevent the juices from running out. Place the oyster in a broiler pan, lined with a layer of salt to keep the shells from flopping over, and repeat with the remainder.

Dry-fry the mustard seeds in a skillet until they start to pop. Add the butter, the shallots, and celery and fry for 3 minutes. Add the garlic and a little salt and pepper and fry for an additional 2 minutes. Stir in the vinegar, Tabasco sauce, and two-thirds of each herb.

Spoon the mixture over the oysters and cook under a preheated broiler for 5–8 minutes, or until the oysters are just firm. Serve sprinkled with the remaining herbs.

For oysters with Bloody Mary dressing, open the oysters as above. Pour their natural juices into a small bowl and place on a serving platter lined with sea salt. Mix 6 tablespoons tomato juice with the oyster juices. Add a squeeze of lemon juice and a dash each of Tabasco and Worcestershire sauce. Stir well and taste for seasoning. Pour a little of the tomato mixture into each of the oyster shells, then sprinkle with a little celery salt. Serve immediately.

cod with roasted tomato toast

Serves **4**
Preparation time **15 minutes**
Cooking time 1¼ **hours**

4 ripe **tomatoes**, halved
a few **thyme sprigs**
2 tablespoons **olive oil**
4 **cod fillets**, about 7 oz each,
  skin on and pin-boned
4 slices of **ciabatta**
1 **garlic clove**
salt and **pepper**

Dressing
large handful of **basil**
4 tablespoons **olive oil**
2 tablespoons freshly grated
  Parmesan cheese, plus
  some shavings to garnish
  (optional)

Place the tomatoes on a baking sheet, season with salt and pepper, sprinkle with the thyme sprigs, and drizzle with 1 tablespoon of the oil. Roast in a preheated oven, 325°F, for 1 hour until soft, then turn the oven up to 350°F. Season the cod and roast along with the tomatoes in the oven for 10–12 minutes, or until the fish is cooked and the tomatoes have softened.

Brush both sides of the bread with the remaining oil. Preheat a griddle pan and griddle the bread until golden brown on both sides. Then rub both sides with the garlic clove.

Place the ingredients for the dressing in a small food processor and blend until smooth. You can also do this using a hand blender.

Top the toast with the tomatoes and then serve with the cod. Drizzle a little of the dressing over the top and garnish with some Parmesan shavings.

For roasted cod & tomato pasta, while the tomatoes and cod are roasting as above, cook 10 oz dried pasta according to the instructions on the package, then drain. Cut the roasted tomatoes into small pieces and flake the cod. Stir through the warm pasta with some of the dressing, prepared as above.

crispy salt cod & chorizo salad

Serves **4**

Preparation time **15 minutes**,
  plus soaking

Cooking time **20 minutes**

1 lb piece of **salt cod**

8 oz **chorizo sausage**, sliced

1 **red bell pepper**, cored,
  seeded, and finely sliced

3 large handfuls of **mixed
  salad leaves**

3 **scallions**, finely sliced

1⅓ cups **frozen peas**, thawed

1 **celery stick**, finely sliced

Dressing

1 tablespoon **wholegrain
  mustard**

1 teaspoon **honey**

4 tablespoons **olive oil**

1 tablespoon **lemon juice**

salt and **pepper**

Soak the salt cod in cold water for at least 8 hours, changing the water as often as possible. Place the soaked salt cod in a saucepan and cover with fresh cold water. Bring to a boil, then reduce the heat and simmer for 5 minutes. Remove the fish and, when cool enough to handle, flake it into large chunks, removing any bones and skin. Set aside.

Heat a large skillet over a medium heat. Add the chorizo and cook for 2 minutes, allowing it to brown. Turn the chorizo slices over and add the salt cod to the pan. Allow both the cod and chorizo to cook until crispy. Remove from the pan using a slotted spoon, leaving behind the excess fat from the chorizo. Fry the red pepper in the chorizo oil for 2 minutes. Remove from the pan.

Mix together the salad leaves, scallions, peas, and celery.

Beat together the dressing ingredients. Add enough of the dressing to coat the salad leaves.

Place the dressed salad on a serving plate and top with the crispy chorizo, salt cod, and red pepper.

For salt cod salad with chickpeas, arugula, & tomato, soak the fish as above, then cut into 2 inch chunks. Heat 1 tablespoon olive oil in a skillet. Add 10 oz halved cherry tomatoes and 1 crushed garlic clove. Cook until softened and starting to break down. Add a 13 oz can chickpeas, drained, and 2 handfuls of arugula leaves. Season with salt and pepper. Heat a little more olive oil in another skillet and fry the cod until crispy. Stir through the tomatoes and chickpeas. Serve with crusty bread.

salmon & watercress roulade

Serves **4–6**

Preparation time **30 minutes**, plus cooling and chilling

Cooking time **25–30 minutes**

3 tablespoons **butter**
6 tablespoons **all-purpose flour**
1 cup **milk**
4 **eggs**, separated
2 cups **watercress**, roughly chopped, plus a few extra leaves to garnish
grated zest of **1 lime**
3 tablespoons freshly grated **Parmesan cheese**
salt and **pepper**
lime wedges, to garnish (optional)

Filling

10 oz **salmon fillet**, pin-boned and halved
¾ cup **sour cream**
2 tablespoons freshly squeezed **lime juice**
salt and **pepper**

Line a 9 x 12 inch roasting pan with nonstick parchment paper.

Melt the butter in a saucepan, stir in the flour, and cook for 1 minute. Gradually mix in the milk and bring to a boil, stirring until thickened and smooth. Remove from the heat and stir in the egg yolks, watercress, lime zest, and salt and pepper. Allow to cool for 15 minutes.

Beat the egg whites into stiff peaks. Fold a large spoonful into the cooled sauce to loosen the mixture, then fold in the remaining egg whites. Spoon the mixture into the prepared pan and ease into the corners.

Bake the roulade in a preheated oven, 350°F, for 15–20 minutes until it is well risen, golden brown, and the top feels spongy. Cover with a clean dish towel and allow to cool for at least 1 hour.

Meanwhile, steam the salmon for 8–10 minutes until it is cooked. Allow to cool, before skinning, flaking, and discarding any bones. Beat the sour cream with the lime juice and plenty of salt and pepper.

Place a large piece of parchment paper on the work surface so that a short edge is nearest to you and sprinkle with the Parmesan. Turn the cooled roulade out onto the paper, remove the pan, and peel away the lining paper.

Spread the roulade with the sour cream mixture, then the salmon. Roll up the roulade, starting from the shortest side nearest to you, using the paper to help. Place in the refrigerator for a least 30 minutes, then cut into thick slices and serve garnished with a few watercress leaves and lime wedges, if desired.

mackerel & wild rice niçoise

Serves **3–4**
Preparation time **20 minutes**, plus cooling
Cooking time **25 minutes**

½ cup **wild rice**
5 oz **green beans**, halved
10 oz large **mackerel fillets**, pin-boned
6 tablespoons **olive oil**
12 **black olives**
8 canned **anchovy fillets**, drained and halved
8 oz **cherry tomatoes**, halved
3 **hard-cooked eggs**, cut into quarters
1 tablespoon **lemon juice**
1 tablespoon **French mustard**
2 tablespoons **chopped chives**
salt and **pepper**

Cook the rice in plenty of boiling water for 20–25 minutes, or until it is tender. (The grains will start to split open when they're just cooked.) Add the green beans and cook for 2 minutes.

Meanwhile, lay the mackerel on a foil-lined broiler rack and brush with 1 tablespoon of the oil. Cook under a preheated broiler for 8–10 minutes, or until cooked through. Allow to cool.

Drain the rice and beans and mix together in a salad bowl with the olives, anchovies, tomatoes, and eggs. Flake the mackerel, discarding any stray bones, and add to the bowl.

Mix the remaining oil with the lemon juice, mustard, chives, and a little salt and pepper, and add to the bowl. Toss the ingredients lightly together, cover, and chill until ready to serve.

For fresh tuna & wild rice niçoise, replace the mackerel with 4 x 7 oz fresh tuna steaks, frying them in a little olive oil for 2–3 minutes on each side so that they are just pink in the center. Complete the recipe as above.

tuna pâté with toasted sourdough

Serves **4**
Preparation time **10 minutes**
Cooking time **5 minutes**

2 x 6½ oz cans **tuna in brine**
3 tablespoons **mayonnaise**
1 tablespoon **tomato ketchup**
2 tablespoons **lemon juice**
1 tablespoon chopped **parsley**
1 **sourdough loaf**, thinly sliced
¼ cup **butter**
1 tablespoon **olive oil**
1 tablespoon **balsamic vinegar**
2 cups **arugula leaves**, washed and drained
2 tablespoons roughly chopped **capers**
10 **sun-blushed tomatoes**, halved
10 **pitted black olives**, halved
salt and **pepper**

Drain the tuna and place it in a small food processor along with the mayonnaise, tomato ketchup, and lemon juice. Blend until smooth, then stir in the parsley and season with salt and pepper. Alternatively, you can make this by hand just mixing the ingredients together. Spoon the pâté into individual pots.

Place the sourdough slices in a preheated griddle pan to toast or under a preheated broiler. Spread with butter.

Mix together the oil and vinegar and lightly dress the arugula leaves. Toss in the capers, sun-blushed tomatoes, and olives.

Serve a pot of the tuna pâté along with the warm buttered toast and arugula salad.

For seared tuna with sun-blushed tomato & olive salsa, season and lightly brush 4 fresh tuna steaks with olive oil. Sear them in a hot griddle pan for 2–3 minutes on each side. Mix together 20 sun-blushed tomatoes and 20 halved pitted black olives with 1 tablespoon baby capers, 1 tablespoon balsamic vinegar, and 2 tablespoons olive oil. Season with salt and pepper and serve with the seared tuna.

gray mullet with pancetta salad

Serves **4**

Preparation time **8 minutes**

Cooking time **10–12 minutes**

4 **gray mullet fillets**, about
  6 oz each, skin on and
  pin-boned
1 tablespoon **olive oil**
7 oz **pancetta** or **bacon**,
  cubed
1⅓ cups **frozen peas**, thawed
2 small **crisphead lettuces**,
  outer few leaves removed
  and cut into 6
a few **thyme sprigs**
3 tablespoons **white wine** or
  water
1½ tablespoons **butter**

Season the fish and steam in a steamer for 4–5
minutes or until the fish has turned opaque.

Heat a skillet over a high heat and add the olive oil. Fry
the pancetta or bacon until crispy, then remove from the
pan and set aside.

Place the peas, lettuce, thyme, and wine in the skillet
and bring the pan up to a low simmer until the lettuce
has softened slighty. Stir in the butter and season with
salt and pepper.

Divide the pea mixture between 4 shallow bowls
and top with the steamed gray mullet and a sprinkle
of crispy pancetta or bacon.

For baby lettuce broth, add 2 cups chicken stock or
Basic Fish Stock (see page 15) to the pan with the
peas, lettuce, and wine. Finish the dish with a sprinkle
of chopped mint. Serve with crusty bread.

tuna with green beans & broccoli

Serves **4**
Preparation time **8 minutes**
Cooking time **15 minutes**

1 lb **new potatoes**
8 oz **fine green beans**, topped
  and tailed
7 oz **tenderstem broccoli**
4 **fresh tuna steaks**, about
  6 oz each
1 tablespoon **olive oil**
½ cup **toasted hazelnuts**,
  roughly chopped
salt and **pepper**

Dressing
4 tablespoons **hazelnut oil**
1 tablespoon **lemon juice**
1 teaspoon **Dijon mustard**

Cook the potatoes, beans, and broccoli in lightly salted water until tender but still with a slight bite to them. Then plunge into ice-cold water to stop the cooking process. Drain and cut the potatoes into quarters lengthwise.

Mix all the dressing ingredients together and season with salt and pepper.

Heat a griddle pan over a very high heat. Season the steaks and rub with oil. Place in the pan and sear on 1 side for about 1 minute, then turn over and sear again for an additional minute (or longer if you want your tuna cooked through rather than pink).

Toss the potatoes, beans, and broccoli in the dressing. Sprinkle with the hazelnuts and serve with the tuna.

For Asian green beans, to serve as an alternative accompaniment, mix together 1 tablespoon sesame oil, 2 teaspoons light soy sauce, 1 seeded and finely chopped chili, 1 teaspoon honey, and 1 tablespoon chopped cilantro. Cook 1 lb topped and tailed green beans in salted boiling water, as above. Drain the beans and, while still warm, toss the dressing with the beans.

salmon with asian coleslaw

Serves **4**

Preparation time **20–25 minutes**, plus chilling

Cooking time **5 minutes**

1 tablespoon **coriander seeds**
1 tablespoon **cumin seeds**
1 lb **thick salmon fillet**, pin-boned and skinned
1 tablespoon **olive oil**
2 cups finely shredded **white cabbage**
1¼ cups grated **carrot**
handful of **sugarsnap peas**, sliced into 3 pieces on a sharp angle
1 **green chili**, seeded and finely chopped
handful of **cilantro leaves**
⅓ cup **roasted cashew nuts**, roughly chopped (optional)
sea salt and **pepper**

Dressing

juice of 2 **limes**
1 tablespoon **sesame oil**
2 teaspoons **palm sugar** or **brown sugar**
1 teaspoon **light soy sauce**
1 tablespoon **Thai fish sauce**

Place the coriander and cumin seeds in a small skillet and toast over a medium heat for a few minutes until fragrant, taking care not to burn them. Lightly crush the spices with a little sea salt and pepper in a mortar and pestle. Rub the spices all over the salmon.

Heat the olive oil in a skillet until smoking. Quickly sear the salmon for 20 seconds on all sides. Remove from the pan and place in the freezer for 20 minutes.

Mix all the dressing ingredients together.

Mix together the cabbage, carrot, sugar snap peas, chili, and cilantro leaves in a large mixing bowl. Add enough of the dressing to coat all the vegetables.

Slice the salmon thinly with a very sharp knife. Cover the base of a large platter with the salmon, pile the Asian coleslaw in the center of the plate, or in a side bowl, and sprinkle with the cashew nuts, if desired.

For Indian-style coleslaw, mix together 2 cups shredded white cabbage, 1¼ cups grated carrot, 1 tablespoon mint sauce, and 6 tablespoons plain yogurt. Season well and sprinkle with a few toasted walnuts. Serve with pan-fried white fish such as red mullet or sea bass.

scallops with morcilla

Serves **6**
Preparation time **10 minutes**
Cooking time **5 minutes**

6 cleaned **sea scallops**,
   preferably in their shells
1 oz **morcilla sausage**
2 tablespoons **olive oil**
1 **scallion**, finely sliced
1 teaspoon chopped **lemon
   thyme**
salt and **pepper**

Pat the scallops dry on paper towels and season lightly with salt and pepper. Finely chop or break the morcilla into small pieces.

Heat the oil in a small skillet and gently fry the scallops for 1 minute on each side. Transfer them to the cleaned shells or to small, warm serving dishes if the scallops were ready-shelled.

Add the scallion, lemon thyme, and morcilla to the pan and heat gently, stirring, for 1 minute. Season lightly with salt and pepper and spoon over the scallops with the cooking juices to serve.

For cilantro dressing, to serve as an accompaniment, whiz ⅔ cup thick Greek or whole milk yogurt with 1 green chili and a large bunch of cilantro in a small food processor. Season with salt and pepper to taste, then spoon over the scallops and morcilla.

baked arbroath smokie soufflés

Serves **4**

Preparation time **10 minutes**,
plus cooling

Cooking time **30 minutes**

2½ tablespoons **butter**, plus
extra for greasing

5 tablespoons **all-purpose
flour**

⅔ cup **milk**

2 **eggs**, separated

5 oz **Arbroath Smokies** or
cooked smoked haddock,
flaked, plus 2 oz extra to
garnish (optional)

⅔ cup **heavy cream**

salt and **pepper**

Lemon Hollandaise Sauce,
to serve (see below)

Melt the butter in a saucepan over a low heat, add the flour, and stir continuously for 1 minute. Remove from the heat and gradually add the milk, beating until smooth. Return the pan to a low heat and bring to a boil, stirring continuously, then reduce the heat and simmer for a minute more. Allow it to cool slightly before beating in the egg yolks. Fold in the flaked fish.

Beat the egg whites until they form firm peaks, then fold them into the fish mixture. Gently spoon the mixture into 4 lightly buttered ramekins or molds (fill them about three-quarters full). Place the filled molds in a roasting pan and fill this with boiling water until it comes one-third of the way up the sides of the ramekins. Bake in a preheated oven, 350°F, for 12–15 minutes, or until set, then remove from the oven and the water and allow to cool.

Unmold the soufflés and place in either individual serving dishes or 1 large dish. Pour over the cream and return to the oven for an additional 10 minutes until hot.

Top with a little more flaked fish before serving with some Lemon Hollandaise Sauce (see below).

For lemon hollandaise sauce, to serve as an accompaniment, melt 1 cup butter in a small saucepan. Place 2 egg yolks and the zest of 1 lemon in a food processor. When the butter is about to boil, turn the food processor on and pour the butter in through the funnel in a steady stream. When all the butter has been incorporated, turn the processor off, add about 2 tablespoons lemon juice, and season with salt and pepper. Blend once more and serve immediately.

thai-style crab cakes with salsa

Serves **4**
Preparation time **20 minutes**
Cooking time **8 minutes**

1¼ lb **fresh white crabmeat**
13 oz **floury potatoes**, cooked
  and mashed
1 inch piece of **fresh ginger
  root**, peeled and finely
  grated
grated zest of 1 **lime**
1 **red chili**, seeded and finely
  chopped
1 tablespoon **mayonnaise**
5 tablespoons **vegetable oil**,
  for pan-frying

Salsa
13 oz can **black-eyed peas**,
  drained
1 **red bell pepper**, cored,
  seeded, and finely diced
10 oz can **corn**, drained
3 tablespoons **lime juice**
2 tablespoons **olive oil**
2 tablespoons chopped
  cilantro
salt and **pepper**

Mix together the crab, mashed potatoes, ginger, lime zest, chili, and mayonnaise. Season the mixture well with salt and pepper. Divide the mixture into 12 portions and shape into cakes with your hands.

Heat the vegetable oil in a skillet and fry the crab cakes for 3–4 minutes on each side until they are golden brown.

Make the salsa by mixing together the black-eyed peas, red pepper, and corn. Squeeze over the lime juice and stir in the olive oil. Season with salt and pepper. Finally, mix in the chopped cilantro.

For salmon & lemon fish cakes, mix together 13 oz cooked and mashed floury potatoes and 13 oz poached and flaked salmon fillet along with the grated zest of 2 lemons and 1 tablespoon mayonnaise. Season well with salt and pepper. Shape the mixture into cakes as above and fry in a little olive oil until crispy.

mackerel & asparagus tart

Serves **4**

Preparation time **20 minutes**, plus chilling

Cooking time **30–35 minutes**

8 **asparagus spears**, trimmed and blanched

8 oz **smoked mackerel**, skinned

2 **eggs**

6 tablespoons **milk**

salt and **pepper**

6 tablespoons **heavy cream**

Pastry

1¾ cups **all-purpose flour**, plus extra for dusting

⅓ cup **lightly salted butter**, chilled and diced

1 **egg**, plus 1 **egg yolk**

Put the flour, butter, egg, and egg yolk in a food processor and blend until a soft dough is formed. If the pastry won't come together, add a drop of cold water. Take the dough out of the processor and knead lightly for 1 minute until it is smooth. Place it in a freezer bag or wrap in plastic wrap and chill in the refrigerator for at least 30 minutes. Alternatively, make the pastry by hand by blending the butter into the flour until it resembles bread crumbs, then working in the eggs.

Roll the pastry out on a well-floured work surface until it is about ⅛ inch thick and line a 10 inch round, fluted tart pan. Trim off the excess pastry. Chill the lined tart pan for 1 hour.

Line the tart with a piece of nonstick parchment paper, cover with pie weights, then place in a preheated oven, 350°F, for 10–12 minutes until lightly golden. Remove from the oven and take away the parchment paper and weights. Place back in the oven for an additional 2 minutes to dry out the base of the pie shell. Remove from the oven.

Slice each asparagus spear into 3 on the angle. Flake the fish into the pie shell and add the asparagus. Mix together the eggs, milk, and cream. Season with salt and pepper. Pour the mixture into the pie shell and cook it in the oven for 20–25 minutes until the mixture has set.

For smoked salmon & pea tart, follow the recipe as above but replace the smoked mackerel and asparagus with 13 oz shredded smoked salmon, 1⅓ cups thawed frozen peas, and 2 tablespoons chopped dill weed. Season with pepper only.

sea bass with sauce vierge

Serves **4**
Preparation time **20 minutes**
Cooking time **5 minutes**

1 tablespoon **olive oil**
4 **sea bass fillets**, about
  6 oz each, skin on and
  pin-boned
arugula leaves
salt and **pepper**

Sauce

4 ripe **tomatoes**, skinned,
  seeded, and finely diced
1 **shallot**, finely diced
2 tablespoons **olive oil**
squeeze of **lemon juice**
a few **basil leaves**, shredded

Mix together the tomatoes and shallot. Add the oil and stir gently to combine. Add enough lemon juice, salt, and pepper to taste. At the last minute before serving, add the basil leaves.

Heat the oil in a skillet over a high heat. Season the sea bass with salt and pepper. When the pan is hot, fry the fish, skin-side down, for 3–4 minutes until the skin is golden brown and crispy. Turn the fish over and cook for a minute more. Remove from the pan and serve with the sauce vierge and arugula leaves.

For salsa verde, as an alternative to the sauce vierge, mix together 5 tablespoons chopped parsley leaves, 1 tablespoon chopped basil leaves, 2 tablespoons chopped mint leaves, 1 teaspoon Dijon mustard, 3 finely chopped canned anchovy fillets, 1 teaspoon chopped capers, and 1 crushed garlic clove. Stir in 6 tablespoons olive oil. Season to taste and serve with pan-fried sea bass or any other fish.

squid with lemon & caper dressing

Serves **4**

Preparation time **10 minutes**, plus marinating

Cooking time **5 minutes**

8 small or 4 large **squid**, cleaned (see page 12) and halved lengthwise, tentacles discarded

2 tablespoons **olive oil**

1 teaspoon **ground cumin**

grated zest and juice of 1 **lemon**

3 tablespoons **white wine**

2 tablespoons **capers**

salt and **pepper**

Open the squid out and pat dry with paper towels. Lay them on a cutting board, shiny-side down, and, using a sharp knife, lightly score a fine diamond pattern on the flesh, being careful not to cut all the way through. Place the squid in a nonmetallic bowl along with the oil, cumin, lemon zest, half the lemon juice, and a little pepper (no salt at this stage). Leave in the refrigerator to marinate for at least 30 minutes, but better still overnight.

Heat a skillet until it is very hot. Add the squid to the pan in batches, scored-side down, and cook for about 1–2 minutes, or until it turns white and loses its transparency. Remove from the pan and keep warm while cooking the rest of the squid.

Return the pan to the heat and deglaze the pan with the wine. Allow the wine to boil for a minute to burn off the alcohol. Remove the pan from the heat and add the remaining lemon juice and finally the capers. Season the squid with salt and pepper and serve with the pan juices poured over.

For mixed herb salad, to serve as an accompaniment, mix together a large handful of parsley leaves with a small handful each of mint and cilantro leaves in a salad bowl. In another bowl, mix together 2 tablespoons lemon juice, 2 tablespoons olive oil, and 1 crushed garlic clove. Pour the dressing over the herb salad.

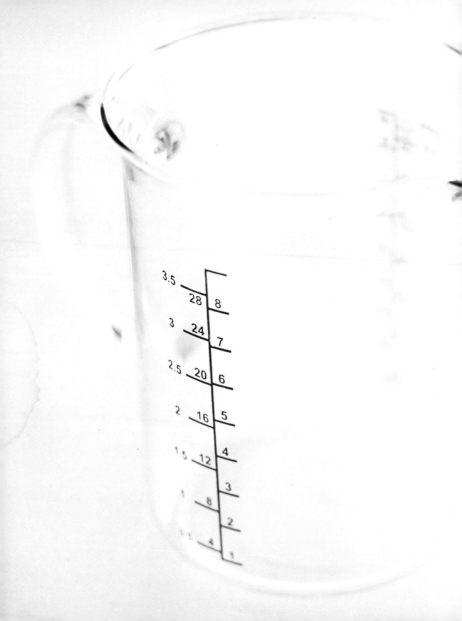

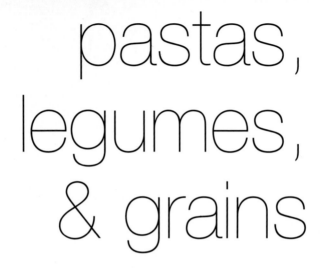

pastas, legumes, & grains

kedgeree with soft-poached eggs

Serves **4**
Preparation time **5 minutes**
Cooking time **18–20 minutes**

¼ cup **butter**
6 **scallions**, chopped
2 tablespoons **mild curry powder**
1½ cups **basmati rice**
1¼ cups **chicken stock**
8 oz **smoked haddock**, skinned and cut into chunks
¾ cup **whipping cream**
3 tablespoons chopped **parsley**
1 tablespoon **white wine vinegar** or **malt vinegar**
4 very fresh large **eggs**
1 **lemon**, cut into wedges
salt and **pepper**
mango chutney, to serve

Melt the butter in a large saucepan over a medium heat. Add the scallions and fry until soft. Add the curry powder and fry for a minute more until fragrant. Add the rice to the pan and stir well.

Pour in the stock and bring to a boil, then simmer for 7–10 minutes, or until the rice is just cooked. Add the smoked haddock, cream, and parsley. Cook for an additional 2 minutes until the fish is cooked and firm. Season with salt and pepper.

Bring a large saucepan of water to a boil. Add the vinegar and a pinch of salt. Stir the water around the pan, then crack the first egg into the center of the spiral of water. Reduce the heat and simmer for 2–3 minutes until the white of the egg is set but the yolk is still soft. Remove from the pan using a slotted spoon and plunge into a bowl of ice-cold water to stop the cooking process. Repeat with the remaining eggs. Once all the eggs are cooked, bring the water back up to a simmer and return the eggs to the water for 1 minute to warm through.

Serve the hot kedgeree with the poached eggs, a wedge of lemon, and some mango chutney.

For homemade mango chutney, to serve as an accompaniment, heat ½ cup white wine vinegar and 1 cup superfine sugar in a saucepan until the sugar dissolves. Add the peeled and diced flesh of 2 mangoes, ½ seeded and finely chopped red chili, 1 crushed garlic clove, and 4 tablespoons lemon juice. Bring to a boil, then reduce the heat and simmer for 30 minutes until it is a jammy consistency. Pour into sterilized jars and seal tightly.

scallops with spiced lentils

Serves **4**
Preparation time **10 minutes**
Cooking time **20–25 minutes**

1¼ cups **split red lentils**
5 tablespoons **olive oil**
2 tablespoons **butter**
1 **onion**, finely chopped
1 **eggplant**, cut into ½ inch
  cubes
1 **garlic clove**, crushed
1 tablespoon **curry powder**
1 tablespoon chopped **parsley**
12 cleaned **sea scallops**,
  corals removed (optional)
4 tablespoons **Greek** or
  whole milk yogurt
salt and **pepper**

Cook the lentils in water according to the instructions on the package. Drain and set aside.

Heat 1 tablespoon of the oil and the butter in a skillet over a medium heat. Add the onion and cook slowly until golden brown, about 10 minutes. When the onion has browned, remove it from the pan and turn the heat up to high. Add another 2 tablespoons of the oil to the pan and fry the eggplant in batches until browned and softened.

Return the onion to the pan along with the garlic, curry powder, and cooked lentils. Fry for a minute more to warm everything through. Season with salt and pepper and finally stir in the parsley.

Heat a skillet over a high heat and add the remaining oil. Season the scallops with salt and pepper. Place them in the skillet and cook for 1 minute on each side.

Serve the scallops immediately with the spiced lentils and yogurt.

For scallops with dhal & spinach, cook 1¼ cups yellow split pea lentils according to the instructions on the package. Drain the lentils and set aside. Fry 1 finely chopped onion in a little vegetable oil with 1 crushed garlic clove. Add 1 teaspoon curry powder, 1 teaspoon garam masala, and a pinch of turmeric to the pan and fry for 1 minute. Add the lentils with a little water or chicken stock to moisten the mixture. Add 1 lb washed baby spinach and stir through until wilted. Cook the scallops as above with a light sprinkle of curry powder on each. Serve with the dhal.

shrimp, zucchini, & pea risotto

Serves **4**
Preparation time **10 minutes**
Cooking time **25–30 minutes**

2 tablespoons **olive oil**
1 small **onion**, finely chopped
1 **garlic clove**, crushed
2 cups **risotto rice**
1 cup **white wine**
about 6 cups hot **chicken stock** or **Basic Fish Stock** (see page 15)
20 **large raw peeled shrimp**
1 large or 2 small **zucchini**, cut into thin disks
1⅓ cups **peas**, thawed if frozen or blanched if fresh
½ cup **butter**
2 tablespoons chopped **mint**
grated zest of 1 **lemon** and juice of ½ lemon
salt and **pepper**

Heat the oil in a skillet, add the onion, and fry until translucent. Add the garlic and risotto rice and fry for 2 minutes, stirring to coat the rice with the oil. Pour in the wine and allow to bubble until just 1 tablespoon of liquid is left.

Add the stock over a medium heat, a ladleful at a time, stirring continuously. Allow each ladleful of stock to be absorbed before adding the next. Keep adding stock until the rice is cooked but still has a slight bite to it. This should take about 15–20 minutes.

Add the shrimp and zucchini just before the last couple of ladles of stock go in. Cook until the shrimp are pink and firm to the touch, about 3 minutes. Finally, stir in the peas, butter, mint, and lemon zest. Season to taste with salt, pepper, and lemon juice.

For red wine & squid risotto, fry 1 finely chopped onion, 2 finely chopped celery sticks, and 2 crushed garlic cloves in a little olive oil. Add 2 cups risotto rice and fry for 1 minute. Pour in 1 cup red wine and bring to a boil, then reduce the heat to a simmer. Add around 6 cups Basic Fish Stock (see page 15) over a medium heat, a ladleful at a time, stirring continuously. Allow each ladleful of stock to be absorbed before adding the next. Keep adding stock until the rice is cooked but still has a slight bite to it. Finally, stir in ¼ cup butter and 1 lb cleaned squid (see page 12) that has been cut into rings (tentacles discarded). Cook for an additional 2 minutes. Sprinkle with chopped chives and serve.

dover sole with bulghur wheat salad

Serves **4**

Preparation time **12 minutes**,
plus standing

Cooking time **2 hours
5 minutes**

2 **red bell peppers**, cored,
seeded, and sliced

16 **cherry tomatoes**, halved

2 **garlic cloves**, thinly sliced

4 tablespoons **olive oil**, plus
extra for greasing

1 cup **bulghur wheat**

2 tablespoons **lemon juice**

1 small **crisphead lettuce**

10 **black kalamata olives**,
pitted

2 tablespoons finely chopped
chives

2 large **Dover soles**, filleted
and pin-boned

salt and **pepper**

Cover the base of a small ovenproof dish with the red peppers and place the tomatoes on top. Season the tomatoes with salt and pepper and stud with the slices of garlic. Drizzle with about 2 tablespoons of the oil and place in a preheated oven, 300°F, for 2 hours.

Place the bulghur wheat in a heatproof bowl and just cover with boiling water. Cover the bowl with plastic wrap and allow to steam for 15 minutes. Drain the bulghur wheat, squeezing out any excess water. Add the lemon juice and some salt and pepper. Keep warm.

Break up the leaves of the lettuce and mix with the roasted red peppers, bulghur wheat, olives, chives, and remaining oil. Carefully stir in the roasted tomatoes, taking care not to break them up too much.

Line a baking sheet with foil. Season the Dover sole fillets and place them on the foil, flesh-side down. Cook under a preheated broiler for 4–5 minutes, then turn the fish over and broil for an additional 2 minutes.

Serve the fish with the warm bulghur wheat salad and a drizzle of olive oil.

For Dover sole with red pepper & tomato sauce,
cook the tomatoes and peppers as above. When cooked, place them in a food processor and blend to form a smooth sauce. Stir in 1 tablespoon olive oil and a handful of basil leaves, roughly chopped. Serve with Dover sole, broiled as above, and sautéed potatoes.

smoked trout & lemon pasta

Serves **4**
Preparation time **4 minutes**
Cooking time **8–10 minutes**

12 oz **dried farfalle pasta**
1 tablespoon **olive oil**
1 **onion**, finely chopped
1 lb **smoked trout**
grated zest of **1 lemon**
¾ cup **sour cream**
2 tablespoons chopped
   dill weed
salt and **pepper**

Cook the pasta according to the instructions on the package.

Heat the oil in a skillet, add the onion, and fry until soft and translucent but not browned. Take the pan off the heat and add the smoked trout, lemon zest, sour cream, and chopped dill weed.

Drain the pasta, reserving 2 tablespoons of the cooking water. Stir the pasta and water into the sauce. Season to taste with salt and pepper and serve immediately.

For garlic & herb bread, to serve as an accompaniment, mix 2 crushed garlic cloves with ⅔ cup softened butter and 2 tablespoons chopped parsley. Slice a baguette in half horizontally. Spread the butter over the bread and place in a preheated oven, 350°F, for 10 minutes until the butter has melted and the bread is crispy.

angler fish & saffron risotto

Serves **3–4**
Preparation time **25 minutes**
Cooking time **30–35 minutes**

1 lb **angler fish**, boned
¼ cup **butter**
1 **onion**, chopped
2 **garlic cloves**, crushed
1¼ cups **risotto rice**
1 glass **dry white wine**
1 teaspoon **saffron strands**
2 teaspoons chopped **lemon thyme**, plus extra to garnish
4 cups hot **Basic Fish Stock** (see page 15)
salt and **pepper**
grated **Parmesan cheese**, to serve

Cut the angler fish into chunks and season lightly. Melt half the butter in a large saucepan and gently fry the onion until it is softened but not browned. Add the fish and cook, stirring, for 2 minutes. Remove the fish with a slotted spoon and add the garlic to the pan. Cook for 1 minute.

Sprinkle in the rice and fry gently for 1 minute. Add the wine and let it bubble until almost evaporated, then add the saffron and lemon thyme.

Add the stock over a medium heat, a ladleful at a time, stirring continuously. Allow each ladleful of stock to be absorbed before adding the next. Keep adding stock until the rice is cooked but still has a slight bite to it. This should take about 15–20 minutes.

Check the seasoning and stir in the fish. Heat through and serve immediately, sprinkled with grated Parmesan and chopped lemon thyme.

For roasted angler fish with saffron sauce, oil a roasting pan and add a 1½ lb piece of oiled and seasoned boned angler fish. Roast in a preheated oven, 400°F, for 8 minutes, or until firm to the touch. Meanwhile, heat 1 tablespoon olive oil in a pan, add ½ chopped onion, and fry until soft. Add 2 crushed garlic cloves and fry for 1 minute. Pour in ½ cup white wine and add a good pinch of saffron threads. Bring to a boil and allow to evaporate completely, then add ¾ cup heavy cream and bring back to a boil. Serve with the roasted angler fish.

spaghetti with mussels & clams

Serves **4**
Preparation time **15 minutes**
Cooking time **15 minutes**

12 oz **dried spaghetti**
2 tablespoons **olive oil**, plus
extra for drizzling
1 small **onion**, very finely
chopped
1 large **green chili**, seeded
and finely chopped
2 **garlic cloves**, finely chopped
1 lb **mussels**, scrubbed and
debearded (see page 12)
2 lb **clams**, cleaned (see
page 12)
¾ cup **white wine**
2 tablespoons **butter**
2 tablespoons finely chopped
parsley
salt and **pepper**

Cook the spaghetti according to the instructions on the package. Drain and set aside.

Heat the oil in a saucepan. When hot, gently fry the onion until soft and translucent. Add the chili and fry for a minute more before adding the garlic.

Increase the heat and add the mussels (first discarding any that don't shut when tapped), clams, and wine. Cover the pan and steam the shellfish until they open, discarding any that don't. Strain through a sieve, reserving the liquid in a bowl.

Return the liquid to the pan, leaving a small amount in the bowl, as this may contain some grit from the shellfish. Boil the liquid for 2 minutes until it has reduced slightly. Beat in the butter, then stir in the shellfish, spaghetti, and parsley. Season well and drizzle with a little olive oil.

For breaded mussels & clams, cook 1 lb scrubbed and debearded mussels and 1 lb cleaned clams (see page 12) as per the recipe above. Remove the top shell of each of the mussels and clams. Mix together 4½ cups fresh bread crumbs with 1 crushed garlic clove and 3 tablespoons chopped mixed herbs. Sprinkle the bread crumb mix over the shellfish and place them under a preheated broiler to brown. Make a garlic butter by mixing together ¼ cup softened butter with 1 crushed garlic clove. Place a small dot of butter on each of the shellfish to melt before serving.

tuna, spinach, & tomato penne

Serves **4**
Preparation time **4** minutes
Cooking time **10** minutes

12 oz **dried penne pasta**
2 tablespoons **olive oil**, plus
    extra for drizzling
1 **onion**, finely sliced
1 **garlic clove**, crushed
1 lb **cherry tomatoes**, halved
pinch of **sugar** (optional)
5 cups **baby spinach**, washed
2 x 6½ oz cans **tuna steak in
    olive oil**, drained
salt and **pepper**

Cook the pasta according to the instructions on the package.

Meanwhile, heat the oil in a saucepan, add the onion and fry gently until soft. Add the garlic and tomatoes and fry for an additional 3–4 minutes until the tomatoes just start to break up. Season the sauce with salt and pepper and a little sugar if it is needed.

Stir the spinach into the sauce. Gently stir in the tuna, trying not to break it up too much, then drain and stir in the pasta. Drizzle a little more olive oil over the dish before serving.

For creamy penne pasta with mussels, cook 12 oz penne pasta according to the instructions on the package. Meanwhile, heat a little oil in a pan and add 1 finely chopped garlic clove, ⅔ cup white wine, and 3 lb scrubbed and debearded mussels (see page 12) to the pan. Cover and cook until the mussels have opened, discarding any that don't. Strain the mussels through a sieve, reserving the liquid. Pour the liquid back into a clean saucepan and add ¾ cup heavy cream. Simmer until it reaches a creamy consistency. Drain the pasta. Pick the mussels from their shells and add to the sauce along with the pasta. Season with salt and pepper.

seafood paella

Serves **4**
Preparation time **30 minutes**
Cooking time **25 minutes**

2 tablespoons **olive oil**
1 large **onion**, finely diced
1 **garlic clove**, crushed
1 **red bell pepper**, cored,
 seeded, and chopped into
 ¼ inch dice
1½ cups **paella rice**
6 cups hot **Basic Fish Stock**
 (see page 15) or **water**
pinch of **saffron threads**
2 large **tomatoes**, roughly
 chopped
10 oz **raw peeled jumbo
 shrimp**
7 oz **clams**, cleaned
 (see page 12)
7 oz **mussels**, scrubbed and
 debearded (see page 12)
7 oz **squid**, cleaned (see page
 12) and cut into rings,
 tentacles discarded
1 cup **frozen peas**, thawed
2 tablespoons chopped
 parsley
salt and **pepper**

Heat the oil in a large skillet. Add the onion, garlic, and red pepper to the pan and fry for a few minutes until they have started to soften, then add the rice and fry for 1 minute.

Pour enough hot stock over the rice to cover it by about ½ inch. Add the saffron threads and stir well. Bring the rice up to a boil, then add the tomatoes and reduce the heat to a simmer. Stir well once again, then simmer for 10–12 minutes, stirring occasionally to prevent the rice catching on the bottom of the pan.

Add the shrimp, clams, and mussels (first discarding any that don't shut when tapped), and squid to the pan, along with a little more water or stock if the rice is too dry. Cook until the clams and mussels open (discarding any that don't), the shrimp are pink, and the squid turns white and loses its transparency.

Stir in the peas and parsley and cook for a few more minutes until the peas are hot, then season to taste with salt and pepper.

For scallop & pasta paella, follow the recipe as above but use 12 oz dried orzo pasta instead of the paella rice, replace the shrimp with scallops, and use only 2 cups stock, adding more only if needed.

swordfish with squash couscous

Serves **4**

Preparation time **15 minutes**, plus marinating

Cooking time **40 minutes**

1 **butternut squash**, peeled, seeded, and cut into ¾ inch cubes

4 tablespoons **olive oil**

1 tablespoon **cumin seeds**

1 teaspoon **ground coriander**

1 teaspoon **ground cumin**

1 teaspoon **paprika**

4 **swordfish steaks**, about 7 oz each and ¾ inch thick

1⅔ cups **couscous**

1 tablespoon **harissa paste**

1¾ cups boiling **chicken** or **vegetable stock**

4 tablespoons **lemon juice**

salt and **pepper**

Place the squash on a sheet pan and drizzle with 1 tablespoon of the oil. Season with salt and pepper and sprinkle with the cumin seeds. Roast in a preheated oven, 350°F, for 30 minutes until the squash is tender.

Meanwhile, mix together the coriander, ground cumin, paprika, and 2 tablespoons of the oil. Rub the mixture over the swordfish steaks and leave in the refrigerator to marinate for 30 minutes.

Place the couscous in a heatproof bowl. Mix the harissa paste with the boiling stock and pour it over the couscous. Cover the bowl with plastic wrap and leave for 5–8 minutes, then fluff the couscous up with a fork to separate the grains. Mix in the lemon juice and remaining oil and season with salt and pepper. Finally, stir in the roasted butternut squash.

Place the marinated swordfish in a very hot griddle pan and cook for 3–4 minutes on each side. Serve immediately with the warm couscous.

For tuna with herb salsa, marinate 4 x 7 oz fresh tuna steaks in a mixture of 1 teaspoon ground coriander, 1 teaspoon ground cumin, a little crushed dried chilies, 1 crushed garlic clove, and 2 tablespoons olive oil. Leave in the refrigerator to marinate for 40 minutes, then cook as the swordfish for 2–3 minutes on each side. Meanwhile, mix together 1 tablespoon each lemon juice, chopped oregano, chopped parsley, and roughly chopped capers, 1 crushed garlic clove, and 2 tablespoons olive oil. Season and serve with the tuna.

noodles with shrimp & bok choy

Serves **4**
Preparation time **5 minutes**
Cooking time **12 minutes**

8 oz **dried medium egg noodles**
3 tablespoons **vegetable oil**
2 tablespoons **sesame seeds**
1 inch piece of **fresh ginger root**, peeled and finely chopped
1 **garlic clove**, crushed
20 **raw peeled jumbo shrimp**
3 tablespoons **light soy sauce**
2 tablespoons **sweet chili sauce**
2 heads of **bok choy**, leaves separated
4 **scallions**, finely sliced
handful of chopped **cilantro**
2 tablespoons **sesame oil**

Cook the noodles according to the instructions on the package. Drain and set aside.

Heat a large skillet and add 2 tablespoons of the vegetable oil. When really hot, add the noodles, flattening them down so that they cover the bottom of the pan. Cook over a high heat for 3−4 minutes until golden brown and crispy. Once they have browned on the first side, turn the noodles over and brown on the other side as well. Stir in the sesame seeds.

Meanwhile, heat the remaining oil in a wok, add the ginger and garlic and stir-fry for 1 minute, then add the shrimp and stir-fry for 2 minutes until turning pink. Add the soy sauce and sweet chili sauce and bring to a boil, then reduce the heat and simmer for 1−2 minutes until the shrimp are pink and firm. Finally, add the bok choy and stir until the leaves begin to wilt.

Place the noodles on a large plate and top with the shrimp and bok choy. Sprinkle with the scallions and cilantro and drizzle with the sesame oil.

For shrimp & lemon grass stir-fry, stir-fry 2 finely chopped shallots, 2 finely chopped lemon grass stalks, 1 seeded and finely chopped red chili, 1 crushed garlic clove and a ¾ inch piece of fresh ginger root, peeled and finely chopped, in a wok in a little vegetable oil for 2 minutes. Add 20 raw peeled jumbo shrimp and stir-fry until pink. Add 6 tablespoons light soy sauce, 2 tablespoons sesame oil, and the juice of 1 lime. Finally, add 2 tablespoons roughly chopped cilantro.

creamy crab & asparagus risotto

Serves **4**

Preparation time **10 minutes**

Cooking time **25–30 minutes**

4 tablespoons **olive oil**

2 **celery sticks**, finely diced

1 **onion**, finely diced

1 **garlic clove**, crushed

1¾ cups **risotto rice**

¾ cup **white wine**

6 cups **Basic Fish Stock** (see page 15) or **chicken stock**

2 tablespoons **butter**

8–10 **asparagus spears**, trimmed, blanched, and sliced at an angle

13 oz **fresh white crabmeat**

3 oz **fresh brown crabmeat** (optional)

1 tablespoon **lemon juice**

2 handfuls of **arugula leaves**

salt and **pepper**

Heat 2 tablespoons of the oil in a large skillet. Add the celery and onion and fry over a medium heat until the onion has softened and become translucent. Add the garlic and fry for 1 minute, then add the rice and fry for 2 minutes, stirring to coat all the grains in the oil.

Pour the wine into the pan and allow to bubble until all the liquid has evaporated.

Add the stock over a medium heat, a ladleful at a time, stirring continuously. Allow each ladleful of stock to be absorbed before adding the next. Keep adding stock until the rice is cooked but still has a slight bite to it. This should take about 15–20 minutes.

Stir in the butter, then the asparagus and the white and brown crabmeat. Season with salt and pepper.

Mix together the remaining oil and the lemon juice and use to dress the arugula leaves. Serve the risotto in bowls, topped with the dressed arugula leaves.

For linguine with crab, chili, & arugula, mix together 12 oz cooked, hot linguine with 3 tablespoons of the pasta cooking water. Add 1 seeded and finely chopped large red chili, 1 lb fresh white crabmeat, 4 tablespoons lemon juice, 13 oz arugula leaves, and 4 tablespoons olive oil. Stir in a few torn basil leaves and season with salt and pepper.

gurnard with parsley risotto

Serves **4**
Preparation time **5 minutes**
Cooking time **25–30 minutes**

4 tablespoons **olive oil**
2 **celery sticks**, finely diced
1 **onion**, finely diced
2 **garlic cloves**, crushed
1¾ cups **risotto rice**
¾ cup **white wine**
6 cups **Basic Fish Stock** (see page 15) or **chicken stock**
1 large bunch **parsley**, finely chopped
grated zest of **1 lemon**, plus the juice to taste
2 tablespoons **butter**
4 **gurnard**, filleted and scaled
salt and **pepper**

Heat 2 tablespoons of the oil in a large saucepan. Add the celery and onion. Fry over a medium heat until the onion has softened and become translucent. Add the garlic and fry for a minute more. Add the rice and fry fo 2 minutes, stirring to coat all the grains in the oil.

Pour the wine into the pan and allow to bubble until all the liquid has evaporated.

Add the stock over a medium heat, a ladleful at a time stirring continuously. Allow each ladleful of stock to be absorbed before adding the next. Keep adding stock until the rice is cooked but still has a bite to it. This should take about 15–20 minutes. Add the lemon zest and stir in the butter. Finally, add the parsley and seaso with salt and pepper.

Meanwhile, heat a skillet over a high heat and add the remaining oil. Season the fish on both sides and place in the pan, skin-side down. Fry the fish on this side for 3 minutes or until the skin is crispy. Turn the fish over and cook for a minute more. Squeeze a little lemon juic over the fish and serve on top of the risotto.

For gnocchi with parsley pesto & gurnard, cook 12 oz gnocchi according to the package instructions. Place a large handful of parsley in a food processor with ½ cup toasted walnuts and 1 garlic clove. Blend with ⅔ cup olive oil until smooth. Add 1¼ cups grated Parmesan cheese and season with salt and pepper. Stir through the gnocchi and serve with the gurnard pan-fried as above.

skate with chickpeas & olive sauce

Serves **4**
Preparation time **15 minutes**
Cooking time **8 minutes**

4 tablespoons **olive oil**
4 **skate wings**, about 8 oz
  each, skinned
3 tablespoons **all-purpose
  flour**, seasoned with salt
  and pepper
1¼ cups **pitted black olives**,
  finely chopped
1 **red chili**, seeded and finely
  chopped
1 tablespoon finely chopped
  basil
1 tablespoon finely chopped
  parsley
2 tablespoons **lemon juice**
13 oz can **chickpeas**, drained
2½ cups **watercress**
1 tablespoon **balsamic
  vinegar**
salt and **pepper**

Heat 2 tablespoons of the oil in a skillet. Dust the skate wings with the seasoned flour and fry for 3 minutes or so until lightly browned. Turn the fish over and cook for an additional 3 minutes on the other side.

Mix together the black olives, chili, basil, parsley, lemon juice, and remaining oil. Season to taste with salt and pepper.

Toss together the chickpeas, watercress, and balsamic vinegar in a bowl.

Serve the skate wings with a handful of the watercress and chickpea salad and the black olive dressing.

For skate with brown butter sauce, heat 2 tablespoons olive oil in a skillet and add the seasoned skate wings. After 1 minute, add ¼ cup unsalted butter to the pan. Baste the skate wing and cook for an additional 2 minutes. Turn the skate wings over and cook for an additional 2–3 minutes on the other side. Continue spooning the butter over the fish. When cooked, add 4 tablespoons drained capers to the pan and season with salt and pepper.

braised pollock with lentils

Serves **4**
Preparation time **15 minutes**
Cooking time **50 minutes**

¾ cup **Puy lentils**
3 tablespoons **extra virgin olive oil**
1 large **onion**, finely chopped
3 **garlic cloves**, sliced
several **sprigs rosemary** or **thyme**
¾ cup **Basic Fish Stock** (see page 15)
4 chunky pieces of **pollock fillet**, skinned
8 small **tomatoes**
salt and **pepper**
2 tablespoons chopped **flat leaf parsley**, to serve

Boil the lentils in plenty of water for 15 minutes. Drain.

Meanwhile, heat 1 tablespoon of the oil in a skillet and fry the onion for 5 minutes. Stir in the garlic and fry for an additional 2 minutes.

Add the lentils, rosemary or thyme, stock, and a little salt and pepper to the skillet and bring to a boil.

Pour into a shallow, ovenproof dish and arrange the fish on top. Score the tops of the tomatoes and tuck them around the fish. Drizzle with the remaining oil.

Bake, uncovered, in a preheated oven, 350°F, for 25 minutes, or until the fish is cooked through. Serve sprinkled with the parsley.

For pollock with braised leeks, heat 1 tablespoon olive oil in a large skillet and fry 4 chopped shallots until golden brown. Pour in 2 cups Fish Stock (see page 15) and ¾ cup white wine, bring to a boil, and reduce by half. Place 4 large trimmed and sliced leeks in a shallow, overproof dish and pour over the reduced fish stock. Season well with salt and pepper. Arrange the pollock on top and bake and serve as above.

main
courses

chili & ginger red mullet parcels

Serves **4**
Preparation time **20 minutes**
Cooking time **6–8 minutes**

4 **red mullet fillets**, about
   7 oz each, pin-boned
2 large **red chilies**, seeded
   and cut into fine julienne
2 inch piece of **fresh ginger
   root**, peeled and cut into
   fine julienne
2 **scallions**, finely sliced
2 **garlic cloves**, sliced
2 **limes**, thinly sliced
1 tablespoon **soy sauce**
1 tablespoon **sesame oil**

Take 4 squares of nonstick parchment paper that are about 3½ inches longer than the fish fillets.

Place a red mullet fillet on top of 1 of the parchment paper squares. Sprinkle with a few julienne of chili and ginger and a few slices of scallion, garlic, and lime. Drizzle over a little soy sauce and sesame oil.

Fold 1 corner of the paper over the top of the fish, leaving you with a triangular parcel. Starting at 1 corner of the triangle, fold the edges in a couple of times to seal the fish in its own packet. Repeat with the other fish fillets. Place in a preheated oven, 350°F, for 6–8 minutes, or until the fish is opaque and firm to the touch.

For lemon & white wine red mullet parcels, place the fish in the nonstick parchment paper as above, laying on a few lemon slices, a few thyme sprigs, and a little butter. Season the fish well with salt and pepper. Wrap the fish in its parcel, leaving 1 end open. Pour 1 tablespoon white wine into each parcel. Close the end of the parcels up and cook as above.

angler fish with balsamic dressing

Serves **4**
Preparation time **15 minutes**
Cooking time **20–25 minutes**

½ cup **balsamic vinegar**
4 **angler fish fillets**, about
  5 oz each, pin-boned
4 teaspoons good-quality
  tapenade
8 **basil leaves**
8 **bacon slices**, stretched with
  the back of a knife
12 oz **green beans**, topped
  and tailed
1 cup **frozen peas**
6 **scallions**, finely sliced
4 oz **feta cheese**, crumbled
2 tablespoons **basil oil**
salt

Pour the vinegar into a small saucepan. Bring to a boil over a medium heat, then reduce the heat and simmer for about 8–10 minutes until thick and glossy. Set aside to cool slightly, but keep warm.

Place the angler fish fillets on a cutting board and, using a sharp knife, make a deep incision about 2 inches long in the side of each fillet. Stuff with 1 teaspoon tapenade and 2 basil leaves. Wrap 2 bacon slices around each fillet, sealing in the filling, and fasten with a toothpick.

Bring a saucepan of salted water to a boil, add the green beans and cook for 3 minutes, then add the peas and cook for a minute more. Drain and keep warm.

Heat a griddle pan over a medium heat and place the angler fish fillets in the pan. Cook for 4–5 minutes on each side until the fillets are cooked. Set aside for 1–2 minutes.

Meanwhile, toss the beans and peas with the scallions, feta, and basil oil, then arrange on serving plates. Top with an angler fish fillet and serve immediately, drizzled with the warm balsamic dressing.

For feta and sundried tomato stuffed angler fish, make an incision into the angler fish, as above, and stuff each fillet with 2 basil leaves, 3 sundried tomatoes, and 1 oz feta cheese. Wrap in bacon and roast as above.

mackerel with sweet potatoes

Serves **2**
Preparation time **15 minutes**
Cooking time **1 hour**

12 oz **sweet potatoes**,
 scrubbed and cut into
 ¾ inch chunks
1 **red onion**, thinly sliced
4 tablespoons **chili oil**
several **thyme sprigs**
15 **sundried tomatoes** in oil,
 drained and thinly sliced
4 large **mackerel fillets**,
 pin-boned
6 tablespoons **plain yogurt**
1 tablespoon each chopped
 cilantro and **mint**
salt and **pepper**
lemon wedges, to serve

Arrange the chunks of sweet potato in a shallow, ovenproof dish with the onion. Add the oil, thyme, and a little salt and mix together.

Bake in a preheated oven, 400°F, for 40–45 minutes, turning once or twice, until the potatoes are just tender and beginning to brown.

Stir in the tomatoes. Fold each mackerel fillet in half, skin-side out, and place on top of the potatoes. Return to the oven for an additional 12–15 minutes, or until the fish is cooked through.

Meanwhile, mix together the yogurt, herbs, and a little salt and pepper to make a raita. Transfer the fish and potatoes to warm plates, spoon over the raita, and serve with lemon wedges.

For fried angler fish with warm sundried tomato dressing, wrap 2 large angler fish fillets in prosciutto ham. Heat a large skillet over a medium heat with 2 tablespoons olive oil. Fry the angler fish for 6–8 minutes until golden brown and firm to the touch. Remove the fish from the pan and allow to rest. Deglaze the pan with 6 tablespoons white wine and the juice of 1 lemon. Stir in 5 drained and chopped sundried tomatoes in oil and 2 tablespoons chopped parsley. Serve the angler fish with the tomato dressing.

indian fish curry

Serves **4**
Preparation time **15 minutes**
Cooking time **30 minutes**

2 tablespoons **peanut** or
   vegetable oil
1 **onion**, finely chopped
1 **red chili**, seeded and finely
   chopped
1 **garlic clove**, crushed
2 inch piece of **fresh ginger
   root**, peeled and finely
   chopped
1 tablespoon **ground cumin**
1 tablespoon **ground
   coriander**
1 teaspoon **turmeric**
1 teaspoon **garam masala**
13 oz can **chopped tomatoes**
1¾ cups **coconut milk**
2 large **angler fish tails**, cut
   into chunks
12 **raw peeled jumbo shrimp**
8 oz **mussels**, scrubbed and
   debearded (see page 12)
small bunch of **cilantro** or
   parsley, roughly chopped

Heat the oil in a large skillet, add the onion, and fry gently for about 10 minutes until golden brown. Add the chili, garlic, ginger, and dried spices and fry for a minute more until fragrant.

Add the tomatoes and coconut milk to the pan. Bring to a boil, then reduce the heat and simmer for about 10 minutes until the curry sauce has thickened. Add the angler fish and shrimp to the pan and cook for 3−4 minutes. Finally, add the mussels (first discarding any that don't shut when tapped) and cook for an additional minute or so until they have opened, discarding any that don't.

Season and stir through the chopped herbs. Serve with basmati rice.

For garlic & black mustard seed naan breads, to serve as an accompaniment, heat a little oil in a small skillet, add 1 tablespoon black mustard seeds and fry until they start to pop. Mix together ½ cup softened butter with the mustard seeds and 1 crushed garlic clove and spread this mixture over 2 large naan breads. Place the 2 buttered sides together and wrap in foil. Bake in a preheated oven, 350°F, for 10 minutes until warmed through.

snapper with carrots & caraway

Serves **4**
Preparation time **10 minutes**
Cooking time **15 minutes**

1 lb **carrots**, sliced
2 teaspoons **caraway seeds**
4 **snapper fillets**, about
   6 oz each, pin-boned
2 **oranges**
bunch of **cilantro**, roughly
   chopped, plus extra
   to garnish
4 tablespoons **olive oil**
salt and **pepper**

Heat a griddle pan over a medium heat and cook the carrots for 3 minutes on each side, adding the caraway seeds for the last 2 minutes of cooking. Transfer to a bowl and keep warm.

Cook the snapper fillets in the griddle pan for 3 minutes on each side. Meanwhile, juice 1 of the oranges and cut the other into quarters. Cook the orange quarters in the griddle pan until browned.

Add the cilantro to the carrots and mix well. Season to taste with salt and pepper and stir in the oil and orange juice. Serve the cooked fish with the carrots and orange wedges. Garnish with extra cilantro.

For carrot & cilantro puree, to serve as an alternative accompaniment to the snapper griddled as above, roughly chop 1 lb peeled carrots. Bring to a boil in lightly salted water and cook until really soft. Drain and whiz in a food processor with 2 tablespoons cream and a little salt and pepper. Once really smooth, stir in 1 tablespoon finely chopped cilantro leaves.

fish pie with crispy potato topping

Serves **4**

Preparation time **20 minutes**

Cooking time **45 minutes**

13 oz **smoked haddock**

14 oz **salmon fillet**, pin-boned
and skinned

5 oz **raw peeled shrimp**

1 **onion**, halved

1 **bay leaf**

a few **peppercorns**

2 cups **milk**

¾ cup **heavy cream**

¼ cup **butter**

3 tablespoons **all-purpose
flour**

salt and **pepper**

Topping

2 large **potatoes**, peeled

2 tablespoons **butter**

¾ cup freshly grated
Parmesan cheese

Place the haddock, salmon, shrimp, onion, bay leaf, and peppercorns in a large saucepan, pour over the milk and cream and bring to a boil, then remove from the heat and allow to stand for 5 minutes.

Remove the fish and shrimp from the liquid and flake the fish into large pieces in a bowl. Set aside. Strain the liquid and discard the flavorings.

Melt the butter in a saucepan over a medium heat, then add the flour and stir well to combine. Cook for 2 minutes, then remove from the heat. Gradually add the strained liquid to the pan, stirring continuously. Return the pan to the heat and continue stirring until the sauce comes to a boil. Simmer for a few minutes, then season with salt and pepper. Pour the sauce into the bowl with the fish and gently stir so that the sauce coats all the fish. Pour into an ovenproof dish.

Cook the whole potatoes in lightly salted boiling water for about 10 minutes until they are almost cooked through. Remove from the water and slice into thin rounds about ⅛ inch thick. Arrange the potato slices on top of the fish and then dot with the butter. Sprinkle the Parmesan over the top and place in a preheated oven, 350°F, for 25 minutes until the potatoes are golden brown.

For lemon new potatoes & peas, to serve as an accompaniment, cook 1 lb new potatoes and 2 cups peas, drain well, and place in a bowl together. Add the finely grated zest of 1 lemon, a large piece of butter, and a little salt and pepper. Toss all the ingredients together.

swordfish confit

Serves **4**

Preparation time **10 minutes**,
   plus chilling

Cooking time **35 minutes**

2 teaspoons chopped **thyme**

3 **garlic cloves**, crushed

½ teaspoon **sea salt**

¼ teaspoon **dried red pepper
   flakes**

4 **swordfish steaks**, about
   7 oz each, skinned

⅔–¾ cup **olive oil**

2 tablespoons **lemon juice**

4 tablespoons finely chopped
   parsley

1 tablespoon **light brown
   sugar**

1 tablespoon **vodka**

Mix together the thyme, garlic, salt, and pepper flakes
and rub the mixture all over the fish steaks.

Place the fish in a single layer in a shallow, ovenproof
dish into which the pieces of fish fit snugly. Pour over
enough oil to just cover the fish. (If the dish is too large,
line it with foil, arrange the fish, and bring the foil up
around the fish so that you don't use too much oil.)
Cover and chill for up to 24 hours.

Bake in a preheated oven, 350°F, for 30 minutes, or
until the fish is cooked through.

Use a slotted spoon to drain the fish, and place on
warm serving plates. Mix together the lemon juice,
parsley, sugar, and vodka with 4 tablespoons of the
cooking juices in a small saucepan. Beat well, reheating
gently, and spoon over the fish to serve.

For sea bass ceviche, cut 10 oz very fresh, skinless
sea bass fillet into ½ inch dice. Place the fish in a
nonmetallic bowl with the juice of 1 lime and 1 orange.
Stir well, cover, and chill for 2 hours. Remove from
the refrigerator, season with salt and pepper, and stir
in 1 finely chopped chili and 2 tablespoons roughly
chopped cilantro leaves.

scallops with tomatoes & pancetta

Serves **4**

Preparation time **10 minutes**, plus cooling time

Cooking time 1½ **hours**

8 small **tomatoes**, halved

2 **garlic cloves**, finely chopped

8 **basil leaves**

2 tablespoons **olive oil**

2 tablespoons **balsamic vinegar**

8 thin slices of **pancetta**

16–20 cleaned **sea scallops**, corals removed (optional)

8 good-quality **canned artichoke hearts** in oil, halved

3 cups **lamb's lettuce**, trimmed

salt and **pepper**

Arrange the tomatoes close together, cut-side up, in a roasting pan. Sprinkle with the garlic and basil, drizzle with 1 tablespoon of the oil and vinegar, and season well with salt and pepper. Bake in a preheated oven, 425°F, for 1½ hours.

Meanwhile, heat a griddle pan over a high heat and griddle the pancetta slices for about 2 minutes, turning once, until crisp and golden. Transfer to a plate lined with paper towels until needed, leaving the pan still over a high heat.

Sear the scallops for 1 minute, then turn them over and cook for 1 minute on the other side until cooked and starting to caramelize. Remove from the pan, cover with foil, and leave for 2 minutes while you cook the artichoke hearts in the pan until hot and charred.

Toss the lamb's lettuce with the remaining oil and vinegar and arrange on serving plates. Top with the artichokes, tomatoes, and scallops, crumble the pancetta over the top, and serve immediately.

For scallop niçoise salad, season 12 large sea scallops, corals removed, and pan-fry in 2 tablespoons olive oil for 1 minute. Turn over and fry for 30 seconds on the other side. In a bowl, mix together 1 cup store-bought marinated artichoke hearts, ⅓ cup pitted black olives, 8 halved cherry tomatoes, and 3 cups lamb's lettuce. Combine 1 tablespoon balsamic vinegar and 3 tablespoons olive oil. Season with salt and pepper, then toss through the salad ingredients. Serve the salad with the scallops pan-fried as above, seasoned with a squeeze of lemon.

sea trout en croûte

Serves **4**
Preparation time **20 minutes**
Cooking time **25 minutes**

2 sheets of **ready-rolled puff pastry**, thawed if frozen
1¼ lb piece of thick **sea trout fillet**, about 14 inches long, pin-boned and skinned
½ cup **soft cream cheese**
3 tablespoons chopped **dill weed**
1 **egg**, lightly beaten
salt and **pepper**

Sauce
1 tablespoon **olive oil**
½ **onion**, chopped
1 **garlic clove**, crushed
3¾ cups **watercress**, thick stalks removed
¾ cup **heavy cream**

Place 1 sheet of the puff pastry on a nonstick baking sheet. Place the fish in the center of the pastry and season with salt and pepper. Mix the cream cheese and dill weed together and spread it over the top of the fish.

Brush the other sheet of pastry with a little beaten egg and place it on top of the fish, egg-side down. Using the side of your hand, push the pastry down and around the fish, enclosing it in the pastry. Trim the pastry to leave a neat border, then lightly push the edges together to form a tight seal.

Score the top of the pastry gently with a knife to create a diamond pattern, then brush with a little more egg. Bake in a preheated oven, 400°F, for 25 minutes until the pastry is golden brown.

Heat the oil in a saucepan and gently fry the onion until soft. Add the garlic and watercress and allow the latter to wilt completely. Pour the cream into the saucepan and bring to a boil. Remove the pan from the heat and carefully blend the ingredients to form a smooth sauce using a hand blender. Alternatively, pour it into a blender and process until smooth. If the sauce is a little thick, add a little more cream or stock. Season with salt and pepper.

Cut the pie into slices or quarters and serve with the watercress sauce.

For smoked salmon en croûte, follow the recipe above, but replace the sea trout with 1¼ lb cold-smoked salmon fillet and add the finely grated zest of 1 orange to the cream cheese.

sesame salmon burgers

Serves **4**
Preparation time **10 minutes**
Cooking time **8 minutes**

8 tablespoons **sesame seeds**
4 tablespoons **black sesame seeds**
4 **salmon fillets**, about 5 oz each, pin-boned and skinned
2 tablespoons **olive oil**
1 tablespoon **toasted sesame oil**
4 **crusty sesame seed rolls**
½ **cucumber**, cut into ribbons with a vegetable peeler
1 small **red onion**, finely sliced

Spread both types of sesame seeds on a large plate, then dip in the salmon fillets so that the top side of each is evenly coated. Heat the olive oil in a shallow skillet and fry the salmon over a medium heat for 4 minutes on each side, or until golden and cooked through. Remove the pan from the heat and drizzle the toasted sesame oil over the top.

Halve the rolls and toast under a preheated broiler. Top each roll bottom with some cucumber and onion, then add a salmon fillet. Finish with the roll tops and serve immediately with extra cucumber and onion.

For sesame & cilantro sashimi, take 13 oz very fresh, skinless and pin-boned salmon fillet. Mix 1 tablespoon each black and white sesame seeds on a plate and cover another plate with finely chopped cilantro. Press the salmon on the sesame seeds, then remove and place the other side on the finely chopped cilantro. Using a sharp knife, cut the fillet lengthwise in half, then cut ¼ inch slices from each piece. Serve with soy sauce.

hake on creamed spinach

Serves **4**
Preparation time **4 minutes**
Cooking time **20 minutes**

4 pieces of **hake**, about
  7 oz each
2 tablespoons **olive oil**
2 **shallots**, finely chopped
1 **garlic clove**, crushed
3 tablespoons **white wine**
1 lb **baby spinach**, washed
6 tablespoons **heavy cream**
¾ cup **pine nuts**
salt and **pepper**

Place the hake in an ovenproof dish, drizzle with
1 tablespoon of the oil, and season with salt and
pepper. Place in a preheated oven, 400°F, for 6–8
minutes or until the fish is firm.

Meanwhile, heat the remaining oil in a large skillet, add
the shallots, and fry gently until softened. Add the garlic
and fry for a minute more. Pour the wine into the pan
and allow to bubble until all the liquid has evaporated.

Add the spinach to the pan in batches, allowing it to wilt
completely, then stir in the cream and season with salt
and pepper.

Toast the pine nuts lightly in a dry skillet over a
low heat.

Place some creamed spinach in the center of each
plate, top with a piece of fish, and sprinkle some
toasted pine nuts over the top.

For pine nut butter, to add to the dish, mix 1⅓ cups
lightly toasted pine nuts with ½ cup softened butter.
Place the butter in a piece of plastic wrap and roll into
a sausage shape. Place in the refrigerator or freezer to
set. When the fish is almost cooked, place a slice of
the butter on top of each piece of fish. Put the fish
back in the oven to finish cooking and let the butter
melt. Serve with the creamed spinach as above.

malaysian swordfish curry

Serves **4**

Preparation time **20 minutes**

Cooking time **20 minutes**

1½ lb **swordfish steaks**, skinned, boned, and cut into chunks

3 **shallots**, 2 roughly chopped and 1 thinly sliced

2 **garlic cloves**, thinly sliced

½ inch piece of **fresh ginger root**, peeled and chopped

¼ teaspoon **turmeric**

1 **red chili**, seeded and chopped

1¾ cups **coconut milk**

6 **curry leaves**

2 teaspoons **palm** or **superfine sugar**

3 tablespoons **vegetable oil**

1 tablespoon **coriander seeds**, crushed

2 teaspoons **cumin seeds**, crushed

2 teaspoons **fennel seeds**, crushed

1 cup **cilantro leaves**, chopped

salt and **pepper**

Season the swordfish with salt and pepper.

Put the chopped shallots in a food processor with 1 of the garlic cloves, the ginger, turmeric, chili, and 2 tablespoons of the coconut milk. Blend to a smooth paste, scraping the mixture down from the side of the bowl.

Scrape the paste into a large saucepan and add the remaining coconut milk, the curry leaves, and sugar. Bring to a boil, then reduce the heat and simmer gently for 5 minutes. Add the fish and cook gently for 10 minutes.

Heat the oil in a small skillet. Add the sliced shallot, the remaining garlic, and the coriander, cumin, and fennel seeds and fry gently for 3 minutes. Stir in the chopped cilantro, spoon the mixture over the curry and serve.

For swordfish & tomato curry, fry 2 teaspoons each fennel seeds, cumin seeds, and coriander seeds in 2 tablespoons vegetable oil for 1 minute. Add 1 finely sliced onion and fry until soft and starting to brown, then add 2 finely chopped garlic cloves and 1 tablespoon chopped fresh ginger root. Fry for 1 minute and add 2 x 13 oz cans chopped tomatoes. Bring to a boil and add 1 teaspoon brown sugar. Stir in 1½ lb skinless, boneless swordfish cut into ¾ inch chunks. Simmer slowly for 10 minutes until the fish is cooked, then season with salt and pepper.

sea bass with lime aïoli

Serves **4**
Preparation time **30 minutes**
Cooking time **8–10 minutes**

4 large **potatoes**, unpeeled
and thinly sliced
4 tablespoons **olive oil**
4 **sea bass fillets**, about
6–8 oz each, pin-boned
salt and **pepper**

Aïoli
4–6 **garlic cloves**, crushed
2 **egg yolks**
juice and finely grated zest of
2 **limes**
1¼ cups **extra virgin olive oil**

To garnish
broiled **lime slices**
snipped **chives**

Make the aïoli. Place the garlic and egg yolks in a food processor or blender, add the lime juice, and blend briefly to mix. With the machine running, gradually add the extra virgin olive oil in a thin, steady stream until the mixture forms a thick cream. Turn into a bowl, stir in the lime zest, and season with salt and pepper. Set aside.

Brush the potato slices well with the olive oil, sprinkle with salt and pepper, and place on a broiler rack. Cook under a preheated broiler for 2–3 minutes on each side or until tender and golden. Remove from the heat and keep warm.

Score the sea bass fillets and brush well with the remaining olive oil, then place them on the broiler rack, skin-side down. Broil for 3–4 minutes until just cooked, turning once. Remove from the heat, garnish with broiled lime slices and snipped chives, and serve with the potatoes and the aïoli.

For sea bass with chargrilled lime vinaigrette, cut a lime in half. Heat a dry skillet until really hot and add the lime halves, cut-side down. Let the lime blacken slightly, then remove the pan from the heat, squeeze the juice into the pan, and add 1 tablespoon honey and 3 tablespoons olive oil. Season with salt and pepper and serve with sea bass fillets, pan-fried for 3 minutes on the skin side and then 1 minute once turned over.

lemon sole with ratatouille

Serves **4**

Preparation time **8 minutes**

Cooking time **30 minutes**

12 small **waxy new potatoes**, scrubbed

2 tablespoons **olive oil**

1 **yellow bell pepper**, cored, seeded, and cut into ½ inch dice

2 small **zucchini**, halved horizontally, then cut into crescents

10 oz ripe **cherry tomatoes**, halved

2 **scallions**, finely chopped

12 **basil leaves**

4 **whole lemon sole**, gutted

¼ cup **butter**

1 **lemon**

salt and **pepper**

Cook the potatoes in salted boiling water. Drain, then rinse under cold running water to stop the cooking process and drain again.

Pour 1 tablespoon of the oil into a skillet over a high heat, add the yellow pepper, and fry for 2 minutes until slightly browned but still crunchy. Add the zucchini and tomatoes and cook until the tomatoes start to break up. Quarter the potatoes lengthwise and add to the rest of the vegetables. Finally, stir in the scallions and basil leaves. Season to taste with salt and pepper.

Place the lemon sole on a baking sheet covered in foil. Season the fish with salt and pepper and drizzle with the remaining oil. Place under a preheated broiler and cook for 5–6 minutes on each side. Dot each fish with a little butter and squeeze over some lemon juice. Serve with the warm ratatouille.

For ratatouille couscous, to serve as an alternative accompaniment to the broiled lemon sole, cook the ratatouille as above but omit the potatoes. Stir this through 2½ cups cooked couscous. Add a large handful of chopped basil leaves and a few pitted black olives.

lemon & ginger scallops

Serves **3–4**
Preparation time **10 minutes**
Cooking time **10 minutes**

1 tablespoon **butter**
2 tablespoons **vegetable oil**
8 cleaned **sea scallops**, corals removed (optional), cut into thick slices
½ bunch of **scallions**, thinly sliced diagonally
½ teaspoon **turmeric**
3 tablespoons **lemon juice**
2 tablespoons **Chinese rice wine** or **dry sherry**
2 pieces of **stem ginger in syrup**, chopped
salt and **pepper**

Heat a wok until hot. Add the butter and 1 tablespoon of the oil and heat over a gentle heat until foaming. Add the sliced scallops and stir-fry for 3 minutes. Remove the wok from the heat. Using a slotted spoon, transfer the scallops to a plate and set aside.

Return the wok to a medium heat, add the remaining oil, and heat until hot. Add the scallions and turmeric and stir-fry for a few seconds. Add the lemon juice and rice wine or sherry and bring to a boil, then stir in the stem ginger.

Return the scallops and their juices to the wok and toss until heated though. Season to taste with salt and pepper and serve immediately.

For ginger, scallion, & cashew nut scallops, fry 1 tablespoon finely chopped fresh ginger root in 1 tablespoon vegetable oil. Add 2 tablespoons oyster sauce and 1 tablespoon water, warm through and then set aside. In another skillet heat a little vegetable oil until really hot, season 8 cleaned sea scallops with salt and pepper and fry for 1 minute on each side, then stir them into the oyster sauce and add 4 sliced scallions and ⅓ cup salted cashew nuts. Serve immediately.

angler fish & sweet potato curry

Serves **4**
Preparation time **15** minutes
Cooking time **18–20** minutes

2 **lemon grass stalks**, roughly
   chopped
2 **shallots**, roughly chopped
1 large **red chili**, seeded
1 **garlic clove**
¾ inch piece of **fresh ginger
   root**, peeled and chopped
3 tablespoons **peanut oil**
3⅓ cups **coconut milk**
2 **sweet potatoes**, cut into
   ¾ inch cubes
2 large **angler fish tails**, cut
   into large chunks
2 tablespoons **Thai fish
   sauce**
1 teaspoon **dark brown sugar**
1½ tablespoons **lime juice**
2 tablespoons roughly
   chopped **cilantro**, to garnish

Place the lemon grass, shallots, chili, garlic, ginger, and oil in a food processor and blend to a smooth paste.

Heat a saucepan over a medium heat and fry the paste for 2 minutes until fragrant, then add the coconut milk. Bring to a boil and cook for 5 minutes until it reaches the consistency of cream. Add the sweet potatoes and cook until tender.

Add the angler fish when the potato has almost cooked, and simmer for an additional 5 minutes, or until the fish becomes firm. Finally, add the fish sauce, sugar and lime juice. Taste and adjust the amounts of these flavorings to taste, then garnish with the cilantro and serve with some Thai sticky rice.

For Thai-roasted angler fish with roasted chili pumpkin, mix 2 tablespoons Thai red curry paste with 4 tablespoons plain yogurt. Marinate 2 angler fish tails, cut into large pieces, in this mixture in the refrigerator for at least 20 minutes, but overnight if possible. Pan-fry the pieces of fish in a little vegetable oil. Cut a 1 lb pumpkin in half, scoop out the seeds, and cut into 1 inch cubes. Sprinkle with dried red pepper flakes and roast in a preheated oven, 400°F, for 15–20 minutes, turning occasionally, until tender. Serve with extra plain yogurt mixed with chopped cilantro.

salmon, shrimp, & spinach pie

Serves **6**

Preparation time **30 minutes**

Cooking time **40–45 minutes**

1 lb 6 oz **puff pastry**, thawed
if frozen

all-purpose flour, for dusting

2 tablespoons **butter**

2 **shallots**, finely chopped

grated zest of **1 lemon**

2 tablespoons **all-purpose
flour**

1¼ cups **light cream**

½ teaspoon **grated nutmeg**

1¼ cups **frozen leaf spinach**,
thawed

1 lb **salmon fillet**, pin-boned,
skinned, and cut into cubes

8 oz **raw peeled shrimp**

1 tablespoon chopped
tarragon

1 **egg**, beaten

salt and **pepper**

Roll out half the pastry on a lightly floured work surface to form a 10 x 14 inch rectangle. Repeat with the remaining pastry. Cover with clean dish towels and allow to rest.

Melt the butter in a saucepan and gently fry the shallots and lemon zest for 3 minutes. Stir in the flour and cook for 30 seconds. Remove from the heat, stir in the cream and then heat gently, stirring continuously, for 2 minutes until thickened. Remove from the heat and season with the nutmeg, salt, and pepper. Cover the surface with plastic wrap and set aside to cool.

Drain the spinach well and season with a little salt and pepper. Lay 1 piece of pastry on a large baking sheet lined with parchment paper and spread the spinach over the top, leaving a 1 inch border at each end and a 2 inch border down each side.

Stir the salmon, shrimp, and tarragon into the cooled cream mixture and spoon over the spinach. Brush the edges of the pastry with water and top with the other piece of pastry, pressing the edges together firmly.

Trim the pastry to neaten and then press the edges firmly together to seal. Brush with the beaten egg and pierce the top to allow the steam out.

Bake on a preheated baking sheet in a preheated oven, 425°F, for 20 minutes, then reduce the temperature to 375°F, and bake for an additional 15 minutes until the pastry is risen and golden.

angler fish wrapped in prosciutto

Serves **4**
Preparation time **15 minutes**
Cooking time **10–15 minutes**

2 large or 4 small **angler fish tails**
12 slices of **prosciutto**
6 tablespoons **white wine**
4 tablespoons **lemon juice**
1 lb **new potatoes**, scrubbed
2 large **mint sprigs**, plus 12 **mint leaves**, finely shredded
2 tablespoons **butter**
2 cups **frozen peas**, thawed
salt and **pepper**

Season the angler fish tails with pepper only and then wrap in the prosciutto. Place the wrapped tails in an ovenproof dish and roast in a preheated oven, 375°F, for 5 minutes. Pour the wine and lemon juice over, return to the oven, and cook for an additional 5 minutes.

Meanwhile, cook the potatoes in lightly salted boiling water with the mint sprigs for 10 minutes, or until tender. Drain, stir in a little of the butter, and season with salt and pepper.

Cook the peas in salted boiling water. Drain the peas and crush lightly with the back of a fork. Stir in the remaining butter and the mint leaves. Season with salt and pepper.

Remove the fish from the oven and cut into 4 or 2, depending on how many tails you have. Serve the roasted angler fish on top of the crushed peas and with the new potatoes. Pour over a spoonful of the cooking juices.

For minted pea & fava bean puree, to serve as an alternative accompaniment for the angler fish when served as an appetizer, boil 1⅔ cups thawed frozen peas and 1½ cups thawed frozen fava beans in boiling water for 1 minute. Drain and place in a food processor with 3 tablespoons heavy cream and a small handful of picked mint leaves. Blend to a smooth puree. Season with salt and pepper.

moroccan fish tagine

Serves **4**
Preparation time **15 minutes**
Cooking time **55 minutes**

1½ lb **firm white fish fillets**,
  such as cod, sea bass, or
  angler fish, pin-boned,
  skinned, and cut into
  2 inch chunks
½ teaspoon **cumin seeds**
½ teaspoon **coriander seeds**
6 **cardamom pods**
4 tablespoons **olive oil**
2 small **onions**, thinly sliced
2 **garlic cloves**, crushed
¼ teaspoon **turmeric**
1 **cinnamon stick**
¼ cup **golden raisins**
3 tablespoons **pine nuts**,
  lightly toasted
⅔ cup **Basic Fish Stock** (see
  page 15)
finely grated zest of **1 lemon**,
  plus 1 tablespoon juice
salt and **pepper**
chopped **parsley**, to garnish

Season the fish with salt and pepper.

Use a mortar and pestle to crush the cumin and coriander seeds and cardamom pods. Discard the cardamom pods, leaving the seeds.

Heat the oil in a large, shallow skillet and fry the onions gently for 6–8 minutes until golden. Add the garlic, crushed spices, turmeric, and cinnamon and fry gently, stirring, for 2 minutes. Add the fish pieces, turning them until they are coated in the oil. Transfer the fish and onions to an ovenproof casserole dish and sprinkle with the golden raisins and pine nuts.

Add the stock and lemon zest and juice to the skillet and bring the mixture to a boil. Pour the mixture around the fish, then cover and bake in a preheated oven, 325°F, for 40 minutes. Garnish with parsley before serving.

For pomegranate & cilantro couscous, to serve as an accompaniment, bring 1¾ cups vegetable stock to a boil. Pour it over 1⅔ cups couscous in a heatproof bowl, cover with plastic wrap and allow to steam for 5 minutes, then stir in the seeds of 1 pomegranate and 2 tablespoons roughly chopped cilantro leaves. Finally, mix in 2 tablespoons olive oil and the juice of ½ lemon and season with salt and pepper.

cod rarebit

Serves **4**
Preparation time **5 minutes**
Cooking time **15 minutes**

2 tablespoons **wholegrain mustard**
3 tablespoons **beer** or **milk**
2 cups grated **cheddar cheese**
2 tablespoons **olive oil**
4 pieces of **cod fillet**, about 7 oz each, pin-boned
salt and **pepper**

Mix together the mustard, beer or milk, and cheese in a small saucepan. Over a low heat, allow the cheese to melt. Stir occasionally and don't let it boil, as the cheese will curdle. Remove the pan from the heat and allow to cool and thicken.

Heat a skillet over a high heat with the oil. Season the fish and place it into the pan, skin-side down. Cook for 4–5 minutes until the skin is crispy, then turn the fish over and cook for a minute more on the other side.

Spread the cheese mixture over the 4 pieces of cod and place under a preheated broiler. Broil until golden brown.

For wholegrain mustard & cream sauce, to serve as an accompaniment to the cod pan-fried as above, in a small saucepan sweat 2 finely chopped shallots and 1 crushed garlic clove in a little olive oil. Add 6 tablespoons chicken stock and ¾ cup heavy cream to the pan and bring to a boil. Stir in 1 tablespoon wholegrain mustard.

sea bream in a salt crust

Serves **4**
Preparation time **15 minutes**
Cooking time **25 minutes**

3½ lb **coarse sea salt**
2½–3 lb **sea bream**
small bunch of **herbs**, such as
   thyme, parsley, and fennel,
   plus extra to garnish
1 **lemon**, sliced, plus **lemon
   wedges** to garnish
pepper
Aïoli (see page 178), to serve

Use foil to line a roasting pan that is large enough to hold the whole fish, and sprinkle the base with a thin layer of salt. Rinse the fish but don't dry it, then place it on top of the salt, diagonally if necessary. Tuck the herbs and lemon slices into the cavity and season well with pepper.

Pull the foil up around the fish so that there is a lining of salt about ¾ inch thick around the fish.

Sprinkle the fish with an even covering of salt about ½ inch thick. Drizzle or spray the salt with a little water and bake in a preheated oven, 400°F, for 25 minutes. To check that the fish is cooked, pierce a metal skewer into the thickest area of the fish and leave for a few seconds before removing. If the skewer is very hot, the fish is cooked through.

Lift away the salt crust and peel away the skin. Serve the fish in chunky pieces and then lift away the central bone and head so that you can serve the bottom fillet. Garnish with lemon wedges and herbs and serve with Aïoli (see page 178).

For sea bream with a herb crust, beat together a large bunch of parsley and 1 tablespoon chopped rosemary with 4½ cups fresh bread crumbs and ⅔ cup softened butter. Season with salt and pepper. Spread the mixture over the skinless side of 4 large sea bream fillets and bake in a preheated oven, 350°F for 10 minutes. Serve with Aïoli (see page 178).

crusted trout with beurre blanc

Serves **4**

Preparation time **7 minutes**

Cooking time **18 minutes**

1¼ cups **fine rolled oats**

3 tablespoons finely chopped
   parsley

1 tablespoon finely chopped
   rosemary

4 **rainbow** or **brown trout**,
   gutted, scaled, and filleted

3 tablespoons **olive oil**

1 **shallot**, finely chopped

2 tablespoons **white wine**

1 tablespoon **white wine
   vinegar**

½ cup **butter**, cubed

1 tablespoon **lemon juice**

salt and **pepper**

Lemon mayonnaise, to serve
   (optional—see below)

Mix together the rolled oats, parsley, and rosemary with a little salt and pepper, and use this mixture to coat the trout fillets. Heat the oil in a skillet. Fry the fish in batches for about 3 minutes on each side, or until crispy and golden brown.

Meanwhile, place the shallot, wine, and vinegar in a small saucepan and bring to a boil, then allow to bubble until just 1 tablespoon of liquid is left. Remove the pan from the heat and beat in the butter a little at a time. The residual heat in the pan will melt the butter. Once all the butter has been beaten in, add the lemon juice and season with salt and pepper. Serve immediately with the trout and Lemon Mayonnaise, if desired (see below).

For lemon mayonnaise, to serve as an accompaniment, place 1 egg yolk in a bowl with ½ teaspoon Dijon mustard. Beat together and gradually add 1 cup light olive oil, beating continuously. When all the oil has been added, squeeze in the juice of ½ lemon and season with salt and pepper. Beat once again.

fish & chips

Serves **4**

Preparation time **25 minutes**

Cooking time **30 minutes**

1 cup **self-rising flour**, plus
   extra for dusting

½ teaspoon **baking powder**

¼ teaspoon **turmeric**

¾ cup **cold water**

3 lb large **potatoes**

1½ lb piece of **cod** or **haddock
   fillet**, pin-boned and skinned

sunflower oil, for deep-frying

salt and **pepper**

crushed minted peas (see
   page 210), to serve

Mix together the flour, baking powder, turmeric, and a pinch of salt in a bowl and make a well in the center. Add half the measurement water to the well. Gradually beat the flour into the water to make a smooth batter, then beat in the remaining water.

Cut the potatoes into ¾ inch slices, then cut across to make chunky fries. Put them in a bowl of cold water.

Pat the fish dry on paper towels and cut into 4 portions Season lightly and dust with extra flour. Thoroughly drain the fries and pat them dry on paper towels.

Pour the oil into a deep-fat fryer or large saucepan to a depth of at least 3 inches and heat to 350–375°F, or until a spoonful of batter turns golden in 30 seconds Fry half the fries for 10 minutes, or until golden. Drain and keep warm while you cook the remainder. Keep all the fries warm while you fry the fish.

Dip 2 pieces of fish in the batter and lower them into the hot oil. Fry gently for 4–5 minutes, or until crisp and golden. Drain and keep warm while you fry the other pieces. Serve with the fries and some crushed minted peas (see page 210).

For tomato chutney, to serve as an accompaniment, roughly chop 2½ lb tomatoes and finely chop 1 onion. Place in a saucepan with ⅔ cup superfine sugar and ⅔ cup malt vinegar, bring to a boil, and simmer gently for 1 hour or until sticky, stirring frequently. Allow to cool and store in sterilized jars.

lemon & sage dover sole

Serves **4**
Preparation time **3 minutes**
Cooking time **30 minutes**

1 lb **new potatoes**, scrubbed
a few **rosemary sprigs**
3 tablespoons **olive oil**
2 **Dover soles**, filleted and
  pin-boned
grated zest and juice of
  1 **lemon**
3 tablespoons **heavy cream**
6 **sage leaves**, finely shredded
salt and **pepper**

Cook the new potatoes in salted boiling water for 6–8 minutes until almost cooked. Drain and place in an ovenproof dish with the rosemary, drizzle with 1 tablespoon of the oil, and season with salt. Roast in a preheated oven, 400°F, for 20 minutes, or until golden brown. Turn the oven off but leave the potatoes in it to keep warm while you cook the fish.

Heat another tablespoon of the oil in a large skillet. Season the fish with salt and pepper and place it, skin side down, in the hot pan. Cook the fish on the skin side for 3–4 minutes, or until the skin becomes crispy. Turn the fish over and cook for a minute more. Remove the fish from the pan and keep warm while you make the dressing.

Put the lemon zest and juice, cream, and sage into the pan and stir well to combine. Add a little water if the sauce becomes too thick.

Pour the sauce over the fish and serve with the roaste new potatoes.

For pan-fried Dover sole with a warm potato & fennel salad, place 1 lb cooked, warm new potatoes in a bowl with 1 finely shredded fennel bulb. In a little oil, fry 1 tablespoon yellow mustard seeds until they begin to pop. Add these to the potatoes. Make the dressing as above, omitting the sage. Pour over the potatoes and fennel, season, and serve with the Dove sole pan-fried as above.

asian swordfish parcels

Serves **4**

Preparation time **20 minutes**

Cooking time **20 minutes**

2 tablespoons **sesame oil**,
plus extra for brushing

4 **shark** or **swordfish fillets**,
about 7 oz each,
pin-boned and skinned

1½ cups sliced **shiitake
mushrooms**

2 oz **sugar snap peas**, halved
lengthwise

1 **mild red chili**, seeded and
thinly sliced

1½ inch piece of **fresh ginger
root**, peeled and grated

2 **garlic cloves**, crushed

2 tablespoons **light soy sauce**

2 tablespoons **lime juice**

2 tablespoons **sweet chili
sauce**

4 tablespoons chopped
cilantro

Cut out 4 x 12 inch squares of nonstick parchment paper and brush the centers of each with a little sesame oil. Place a piece of fish in the center of each square. Mix together the mushrooms, sugar snap peas and chili and pile on top of the fish.

Mix together the remaining oil, ginger, and garlic and spoon over the vegetables. Bring the sides of the paper up over the fish as though wrapping a parcel. Fold the edges together and flatten gently.

Flatten the ends and fold them over to seal. Place the parcels on a baking sheet and bake in a preheated oven, 375°F, for 20 minutes. Open 1 of the parcels and test whether the fish is cooked through. If necessary, return to the oven for a few more minutes.

Meanwhile, mix together the soy sauce, lime juice, sweet chili sauce, and cilantro. Loosen the parcels and spoon the dressing over the fish before serving.

For Asian mussel parcels, divide 2 lb cleaned mussels (see page 12), 1 finely chopped red chili, 1 inch piece of finely chopped fresh ginger root, and 1 chopped garlic clove between 4 large squares of nonstick parchment paper. Mix ½ cup coconut milk and 1 tablespoon Thai fish sauce, season, and divide between the mussels; fold over the edges of the paper to seal the parcels. Bake in a preheated oven, 400°F, for 6–8 minutes. Check 1 parcel to see if the mussels are open; if not, return to the oven for a few more minutes. Sprinkle with a little chopped cilantro and serve with bread.

sea bream with fennel & vermouth

Serves **4**
Preparation time **4 minutes**
Cooking time **25 minutes**

¼ cup **butter**
3 tablespoons **olive oil**
2 **fennel bulbs**, cut into
   8, herby tops reserved
3 tablespoons **dry vermouth**
4 tablespoons **water**
2 teaspoons **fennel seeds**
1 **dried red chili**
4 **sea bream fillets**, about
   7 oz each, pin-boned
8 **sun-blushed tomatoes**,
   finely chopped in a little of
   their own oil
1 tablespoon **thick balsamic
   vinegar**
salt and **pepper**

Heat the butter and 1 tablespoon of the oil in a shallow sauté pan. Put the fennel in the pan and fry until golden brown on 1 side. Add the vermouth and measurement water, then cover and cook over a low heat or in a preheated oven, 325°F, for 20 minutes, or until the fennel is tender. You may need to add a little more water if the pan becomes too dry.

Heat a skillet, add the fennel seeds and chili, and fry for 1 minute until fragrant. Crush them using a mortar and pestle until the chili has broken up and the fennel seeds are lightly crushed.

Score the skin of the fish and drizzle with a little oil. Sprinkle with the crushed fennel seeds and chili. Season the fish with salt and pepper. Heat the remaining oil in a hot skillet and place the fish in the pan, skin-side down. Fry the fish for about 4 minutes, or until the skin is crispy, then turn the fish over and cook for a minute more on the other side.

Place the braised fennel in the center of the plate and top with the fish. Sprinkle over the reserved herby tops of the fennel and drizzle with a little of the sun-blushed tomatoes, vinegar, and any braising juices.

For crunchy fennel salad, to serve as an alternative accompaniment, use a very sharp knife to finely slice 2 fennel bulbs and 10 radishes. Drop them into ice-cold water for 10 minutes to get really crispy, then remove and drain well. Mix together 1 seeded and finely chopped red chili, the juice of 1 lime, and 3 tablespoons olive oil, and dress the salad. Serve with sea bream and a drizzle of thick balsamic vinegar.

chorizo-stuffed flounder

Serves **4**
Preparation time **20 minutes**
Cooking time **20–25 minutes**

4 oz **chorizo sausage**
1 cup **fresh bread crumbs**
2 tablespoons **sundried tomato paste**
5 tablespoons **olive oil**
2 large **flounder**, cut into 8 fillets, pin-boned, and skinned
8 small ripe **tomatoes** or 4 large tomatoes, halved
several **thyme sprigs**
splash of **white wine**
salt and **pepper**

Cut the chorizo into pieces and process in a food processor until it is finely chopped. Alternatively, chop it finely with a knife. Add the bread crumbs, tomato paste and 1 tablespoon of the oil and blend until combined.

Lay the flounder fillets, skinned-side up, on the work surface. Spread each with a thin layer of the chorizo mixture and roll up, starting from the thick end.

Put the fish in a large, shallow, ovenproof dish and tuck the tomatoes and thyme around the fish. Drizzle with the remaining oil and the wine and season the fish lightly with salt and pepper.

Bake in a preheated oven, 400°F, for 20–25 minutes, or until cooked through.

For herby flounder roll-ups with tapenade, spread 1 tablespoon black olive tapenade over 1 side of 4 skinned and pin-boned flounder fillets. Mix 1 tablespoon each chopped mint and parsley and the grated zest of 1 lemon and season with salt and pepper. Sprinkle over the tapenade. Roll up the fish, starting at the thick end, and secure with a toothpick. Place the rolls in an ovenproof dish and roast in a preheated oven, 350°F, for 8 minutes.

salmon with horseradish crust

Serves **4**
Preparation time **10 minutes**
Cooking time **20 minutes**

4 **salmon fillets**, about
  7 oz each, skin on and
  pin-boned
4 tablespoons **mild**
  horseradish sauce
2 cups **fresh bread crumbs**
20 **asparagus spears**,
  trimmed
1 tablespoon **olive oil**
4–5 tablespoons **sour cream**
4 tablespoons **lemon juice**
1 tablespoon chopped **parsley**
salt and **pepper**

Place the salmon fillets in an ovenproof dish, skin-side down. Spread the top of each fillet with 1 tablespoon of the horseradish sauce, then sprinkle with the bread crumbs. Place in a preheated oven, 350°F, for 12–15 minutes until the fish is cooked and the bread crumbs are golden brown.

Meanwhile, blanch the asparagus in salted boiling water for 2 minutes. Drain and place in a very hot griddle pan with the oil to char slightly. Season with salt and pepper.

Mix together the sour cream, lemon juice, and parsley and season with salt and pepper.

Serve the salmon with the chargrilled asparagus and lemon sour cream.

For roasted salmon with horseradish sauce, season the salmon with salt and pepper and roast in the oven as above. Add a finely chopped shallot to a little olive oil in a pan and cook until softened. Remove from the heat and add 2 tablespoons horseradish sauce and 6 tablespoons sour cream. Season with salt and pepper. Serve with the roasted salmon.

breaded hake & crushed pea rolls

Serves **2**
Preparation time **12 minutes**
Cooking time **10–12 minutes**

⅔ cup **frozen petits pois**
2 tablespoons **butter**
2½ tablespoons **mint**, finely
   chopped
½ cup **fresh bread crumbs**
finely grated zest of 1 **lemon**
4 tablespoons **parsley**,
   chopped
1 **egg**, lightly beaten
2 **hake fillets**, about 4 oz
   each, pin-boned
5 tablespoons **vegetable oil**
2 large **soft, floured rolls**,
   halved horizontally
salt and **pepper**
tartare sauce, to serve

Cook the peas in boiling water for about 4 minutes until soft. Drain and return to the saucepan with the butter and some salt and pepper. Use a potato masher to crush the peas so that they are almost pureed. Stir in the mint and set aside.

Mix the bread crumbs with the lemon zest, some salt and pepper, and the parsley, and spread on a large plate. Pour the beaten egg into a shallow bowl and dip the hake fillets into it before placing them on the bread crumbs. Turn the fish in the bread crumbs, making sure the flesh is completely covered.

Heat the oil in a skillet over a medium-high heat and add the fish to the pan. Cook for about 4 minutes, turning once, until the fish is cooked through and the bread crumbs are golden and crispy.

Spread the crushed peas over the bases of the rolls and lay the fish on top. Top with the lids, then toast in a sandwich grill for 2–3 minutes, or according to the manufacturer's instructions, until the bread is golden and crispy. Cut each sandwich into quarters and serve immediately with tartare sauce.

For breaded hake & tangy coleslaw rolls, cook the hake as above. Meanwhile, coarsely grate 2 carrots and finely shred 4 oz each white and red cabbage. Place in a bowl and add the grated zest of 1 lemon, 1 teaspoon Dijon mustard, 1 tablespoon mayonnaise, and 1 tablespoon sour cream. Season with salt and pepper and a dash of Tabasco sauce. Place the hake in toasted rolls and top with the coleslaw.

caramelized onion & anchovy tart

Serves **4**

Preparation time **25 minutes**,
plus chilling

Cooking time **45 minutes**

2 tablespoons **butter**

2 tablespoons **olive oil**

3 large **onions**, finely sliced

2 **thyme sprigs**

2 **eggs**

6 tablespoons **milk**

6 tablespoons **heavy cream**

2 **tomatoes**, thinly sliced

8 **canned anchovy fillets**,
drained

salt and **pepper**

Pastry

1¾ cups **all-purpose flour**,
plus extra for dusting

⅓ cup lightly salted **butter**,
chilled and diced

1 **egg**, plus 1 **egg yolk**

Put the flour, butter, egg, and egg yolk in a food processor and blend until a soft dough is formed. If the pastry will not come together, add a drop of cold water. Take the dough out of the processor and knead lightly until smooth. Place it in a freezer bag or wrap in plastic wrap and chill in the refrigerator for at least 30 minutes.

Roll the pastry out on a well-floured work surface until it is about ⅛ inch thick and use to line a 9 inch fluted tart pan. Trim off the excess pastry. Chill the lined tart pan for 1 hour.

Line the tart with a piece of nonstick parchment paper and cover with pie weights, then place in a preheated oven, 350°F, for 10−12 minutes until lightly golden. Remove from the oven and take away the parchment paper and pie weights. Place back in the oven for an additional 2 minutes to dry out the base of the tart shell. Remove from the oven once more and set aside. Leave the oven on.

Meanwhile, heat the butter and oil in a skillet, add the onions and thyme, and fry over a low heat for about 20 minutes until the onions are golden brown.

Remove the thyme and spread the onions over the tart base. Beat together the eggs, milk, and cream in a bowl, season with salt and pepper, and pour over the onions. Cook in the oven for 10 minutes until slightly risen and starting to set. Remove from the oven and arrange the tomatoes and anchovies on top of the tart, then return it the oven for an additional 10−15 minutes until the filling has set completely. Cool for 5 minutes before serving.

crab burgers

Serves **4**
Preparation time **15 minutes**
Cooking time **20–30 minutes**

2 tablespoons **olive oil**
1 **onion**, chopped
2 **green bell peppers**, cored, seeded, and finely chopped
2 **garlic cloves**, crushed
½ bunch of **scallions**, finely chopped
2 cups **fresh bread crumbs**
8 oz **fresh white** and **brown crabmeat**
1 tablespoon **Worcestershire sauce**
½ teaspoon **cayenne pepper**
3 tablespoons chopped **parsley**
1 **egg**, beaten
sunflower oil, for pan-frying
salt
iceberg lettuce, to serve
ready-made tomato relish, to serve (optional)

Heat the olive oil in a skillet and gently fry the onion and green peppers for 5 minutes, or until softened. Add the garlic and scallions and fry for an additional 5 minutes. Tip into a bowl.

Add the bread crumbs, crabmeat, Worcestershire sauce, cayenne, parsley, and beaten egg and season with a little salt. Mix well with a wooden spoon, or with your hands, until the mixture is evenly combined.

Divide the mixture into 4 equal pieces and shape each into a ball. Flatten into a burger shape.

Heat a very thin layer of sunflower oil in a large skillet. Fry the burgers (if necessary in 2 batches) for 4–5 minutes on each side until golden. Serve the burgers on a bed of lettuce, topped with tomato relish, if desired.

For crab quesadillas, brush 1 side of 2 flour tortillas with a little vegetable oil. Mix 8 oz fresh white crabmeat with 2 tablespoons mayonnaise, season with salt and pepper, then add 1 tablespoon chopped tarragon. Mix well. Spread this over the unoiled side of the 2 flour tortillas. Slice 2 tomatoes and place on the crab mixture. Top each with another flour tortilla. Brush the top with a little oil. Heat a dry skillet over a high heat, then fry on both sides of each quesadilla for 1 minute, or until golden. Cut each quesadilla into 6 pieces and serve with an arugula salad.

salmon with asian greens

serves **4**

preparation time **15 minutes**

cooking time **25 minutes**

4 chunky **salmon steaks**,
about 7 oz each
vegetable oil, for oiling
1 tablespoon **tamarind paste**
2–3 tablespoons **soy sauce**
½ inch piece of **fresh ginger
root**, grated
2 teaspoons **superfine sugar**
2 **garlic cloves**, crushed
1 **mild green chilli**, finely
sliced
1 teaspoon **cornstarch**
8 oz **bok choy**
8 **scallions**, halved lengthwise
¾ cup **fresh cilantro**, chopped

Put the salmon steaks on an oiled roasting rack or wire rack inside a roasting pan and pour 1¾ cups boiling water into the pan. Cover tightly with foil and cook in a preheated oven, 350°F, for 15 minutes, or until the salmon is almost cooked through.

Meanwhile, put the tamarind in a small saucepan and blend in ¾ cup water. Stir in the soy sauce, ginger, sugar, garlic, and chili and heat through gently for 5 minutes. Blend the cornstarch with 1 tablespoon water and add to the pan. Heat gently, stirring, for 1–2 minutes, or until thickened.

Quarter the bok choy lengthwise into wedges and arrange the pieces around the salmon on the rack with the scallions. Re-cover and return to the oven for an additional 8–10 minutes, or until the vegetables have wilted.

Stir the cilantro into the sauce. Transfer the fish and greens to warm serving plates, pour over the sauce, and serve.

For salmon with chili and ginger bok choy, heat 2 tablespoons of sesame oil in a wok over a high heat and fry 1 finely chopped chili and a ½ inch piece of finely chopped ginger. Add the leaves of 3 heads of bok choy and stir-fry for a minute or until the leaves have wilted. Stir in 2 tablespoons of soy sauce and serve with the salmon.

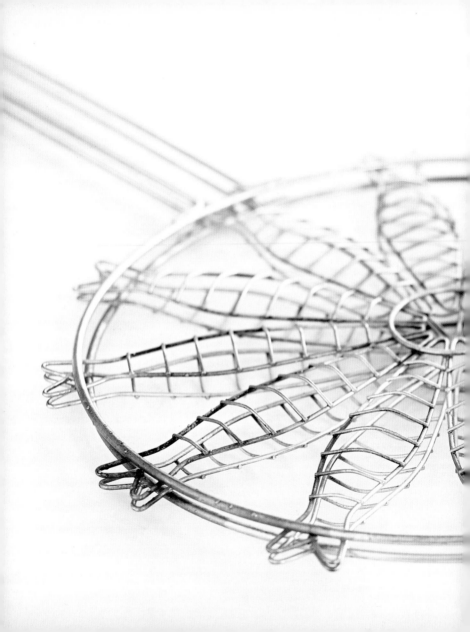

barbecue

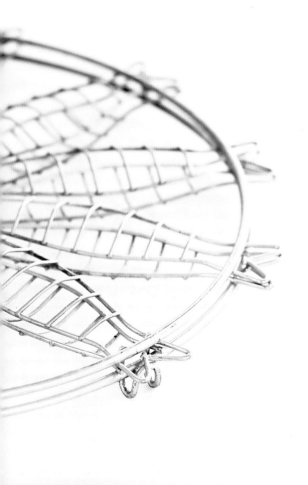

lime & cilantro sea bass

Serves **4**

Preparation time **20 minutes**, plus chilling

Cooking time **10 minutes**

⅔ cup **butter**, softened

3 tablespoons chopped **cilantro**, plus small bunch

1 large **red chili**, seeded and finely chopped

2 **limes**

4 whole **sea bass**, gutted and scaled

2 tablespoons **vegetable oil**

salt and **pepper**

Mix together the butter, chopped cilantro, chili, and add the grated zest of the limes. Season with salt and pepper. Take a sheet of plastic wrap and spoon the butter mixture onto it. Roll the plastic wrap up to form a sausage. Twist the ends of the sausage to enclose the butter and place it in the refrigerator to set.

Take the fish and make 3 slits in the flesh on each side making sure you don't cut all the way through it. Slice the zested limes and place a few slices of lime in the cavity of each fish, along with some cilantro sprigs.

Brush the outside of the fish lightly with the oil and season both sides generously with salt and pepper.

Place the fish either directly on the rack of a medium-hot barbecue or place it in a fish grill first (this is easier). Cook the fish for 5 minutes on each side. The best way to test if the fish is cooked is by looking inside the cavity to see if the flesh has become opaque or if the fish is firm to the touch.

Slice the butter thinly into rounds and place a slice in each of the cuts you made on 1 side of the fish. Allow the butter to melt. Serve with a green salad.

For barbecued sea bass parcels, butter 4 large square pieces of foil and place a sea bass in the center of each piece. Drizzle over a little olive oil and place a few pieces of chopped chili and ginger and a couple of slices of lime in each parcel. Seal the parcels and place them on a medium-hot barbecue for 8–10 minutes, or until the fish turns opaque.

lemon grass shrimp skewers

Serves **4**
Preparation time **10 minutes**,
   plus marinating
Cooking time **8 minutes**

5 **lemon grass stalks**
4 tablespoons **sweet chili**
   sauce, plus extra to serve
2 tablespoons chopped
   cilantro
2 tablespoons **sesame oil**
20 **raw jumbo shrimp**, peeled
   but tails left on

Take 1 of the lemon grass stalks and remove the outer leaves. Finely slice it and place it in a bowl along with the sweet chili sauce, cilantro, and oil. Place the shrimp in this marinade, cover, and leave in the refrigerator to marinate for 1 hour or overnight.

Remove the shrimp from the marinade. Take the remaining 4 lemon grass stalks and remove a few of the outer layers to give you a thin lemon grass skewer. Make a hole through each shrimp at its thickest part using a metal skewer, then thread 5 of the shrimp on to a lemon grass stalk. Repeat with the remaining lemon grass and shrimp.

Place the shrimp skewers on a barbecue and cook for 4 minutes on each side, or until the shrimp have turned pink and are firm to the touch.

Serve the shrimp straight from the barbecue with sweet chili sauce for dipping.

For cilantro sauce, to serve with simple barbecued shrimp, place a large handful of cilantro leaves in a food processor and blend with ¾ cup plain yogurt. Add 1 teaspoon mint sauce and season with salt and pepper.

piri piri swordfish with tomato salsa

Serves **4**

Preparation time **7 minutes**, plus marinating

Cooking time **11–16 minutes**

2 tablespoons **piri piri seasoning**

2 tablespoons **olive oil**

4 **swordfish steaks**, about 7 oz each

6 ripe **plum tomatoes**, halved

1 tablespoon finely chopped **parsley**

1 tablespoon finely chopped **basil**

1 **green chili**, seeded and finely chopped

grated zest of **1 lemon**, plus a little juice

salt and **pepper**

lemon wedges, to serve

Mix the piri piri seasoning with 1 tablespoon of the oil and rub it over the swordfish steaks. Leave in the refrigerator to marinate for 30 minutes.

Place the tomatoes on a hot barbecue until they blacken slightly and become soft. This should take around 5–8 minutes. Remove, roughly chop, and allow to cool slightly. Stir in the parsley, basil, chili, and lemon zest. Finally, add a little lemon juice and the remaining oil and season with salt and pepper.

Place the marinated swordfish on the barbecue and cook for 3–4 minutes on each side. Serve with the charred tomato salsa and lemon wedges.

For barbecued pepper relish, to serve as an alternative accompaniment, core, seed, and chop 1 red, 1 yellow, and 1 orange bell pepper into large chunks. Rub the peppers with a little olive oil mixed with 1 tablespoon piri piri seasoning. Place the peppers on a hot barbecue and cook until they have blackened slightly and become really soft, then remove, chop the chunks into smaller pieces, and mix with a little more olive oil, a little lime juice, 1 tablespoon chopped cilantro, and 1 seeded and finely chopped red chili. Season with salt and pepper.

spiced mackerel fillets

Serves **4**
Preparation time **4 minutes**
Cooking time **5–6 minutes**

2 tablespoons **olive oil**
1 tablespoon **smoked paprika**
1 teaspoon **cayenne pepper**
4 **mackerel**, scaled, filleted,
  and pin-boned
2 **limes**, quartered
salt and **pepper**

Mix together the oil, paprika, and cayenne with a little salt and pepper. Make 3 shallow cuts in the skin of the mackerel and brush over the spiced oil.

Place the lime quarters and mackerel on a hot barbecue, skin-side down first, and cook for 4–5 minutes until the skin is crispy and the limes are charred. Turn the fish over and cook for a minute more on the other side. Serve with an arugula salad.

For mackerel with black pepper & bay, mix together 4 very finely shredded bay leaves, 1 crushed garlic clove, ½ teaspoon pepper, a pinch of salt, and 4 tablespoons olive oil. Rub the marinade over and into the cavity of 4 gutted and scaled mackerel. Place them on a very hot barbecue and cook for 3–4 minutes on each side.

sardines & greek salad bruschetta

Serves **4**
Preparation time **15 minutes**
Cooking time **6–8 minutes**

8 **fresh sardines**, gutted and
    scaled
2 tablespoons **olive oil**
4 thick slices of **ciabatta**
    bread
1 **garlic clove**, peeled
salt and **pepper**

Greek salad

4 **tomatoes**, cut into 8 pieces
    each
½ **cucumber**, seeded and cut
    into ½ inch chunks
10 **pitted black olives**, halved
7 oz **feta cheese**, cut into
    ½ inch cubes
1 tablespoon **lemon juice**
2 tablespoons **olive oil**
10 **mint leaves**, finely
    shredded

Combine all the Greek salad ingredients and season with pepper. Set aside while you cook the sardines.

Brush the sardines with a little of the oil and season well with salt and pepper. Place the fish on a hot barbecue and cook for 3–4 minutes on each side, or until the fish is firm to the touch.

Drizzle the slices of ciabatta with the remaining oil and place on the barbecue to toast. When they are toasted rub both sides with the garlic clove.

Top the ciabatta with the Greek salad and serve with the warm barbecued sardines.

For lemon, garlic, & rosemary sardines, mix together 4 tablespoons olive oil, the grated zest of 1 lemon, 1 tablespoon finely chopped rosemary, 2 thinly sliced garlic cloves, and some salt and pepper. Brush 8 gutted and scaled sardines with a little of this oil and place on a hot barbecue for 3 minutes on each side. Keep brushing the sardines as they cook. Serve with a simple green salad and a little lemon juice squeezed over.

scallops wrapped in prosciutto

Serves **4**
Preparation time **15 minutes**
Cooking time **4 minutes**

6 slices of **prosciutto**
12 cleaned **sea scallops**,
   corals removed (optional)
4 long **rosemary sprigs**
1 tablespoon **olive oil**
green salad leaves
salt and **pepper**

Dressing
4 tablespoons **lemon juice**,
   plus extra to serve
1 **garlic clove**, crushed
1 tablespoon **white wine**
   vinegar
3 tablespoons **olive oil**
1 teaspoon **Dijon mustard**

Cut the slices of prosciutto in half horizontally. Wrap half a slice around the outside of each scallop.

Thread 3 of the scallops onto a metal skewer, alternating with the corals if using. Once the holes have been made in each scallop, remove the metal skewers and strip the rosemary sprigs of their leaves, leaving just a tuft at the end. Thread the scallops onto the rosemary skewers.

Season the scallops with pepper only. Drizzle the scallops with the oil and cook on a hot barbecue for 2 minutes on each side.

Place the dressing ingredients in a bowl and beat together. Season to taste with salt and pepper. Use to dress the salad leaves and serve with the scallops, seasoned with a squeeze of lemon juice.

For scallop, chorizo, & red pepper skewers, thread slices of chorizo sausage and pieces of red bell pepper along with 2 cleaned scallops onto presoaked bamboo skewers. Season with salt and pepper, then place on a hot barbecue for 5 minutes, turning occasionally, until the chorizo is cooked.

thai red snapper with mango salsa

Serves **4**

Preparation time **20 minutes**,
  plus marinating

Cooking time **8 minutes**

4 **red snappers**, gutted and
  scaled

Curry paste

2 tablespoons **vegetable oil**

2 large **green chilies**

2 **lemon grass stalks**, roughly
  chopped

1 inch piece of **fresh ginger
  root**, peeled and chopped

1 **garlic clove**

2 **shallots**, peeled

1 teaspoon **brown sugar**

grated zest of **1** lime

Salsa

2 ripe **mangoes**, peeled and
  cut into ½ inch dice

1 **red chili**, seeded and finely
  chopped

½ **red onion**, finely sliced

3 tablespoons **lime juice**

2 tablespoons roughly
  chopped **cilantro**

1 tablespoon **olive oil**

Place all the ingredients for the curry paste in a small food processor and blend to a smooth paste.

Make 3 cuts in the skin of the fish on both sides. Place the fish in a nonmetallic dish and pour over the marinade, making sure it gets into the cavity of the fish as well. Allow to marinate in the refrigerator for a minimum of 1 hour, but ideally 3–4 hours.

Place the fish on a medium-hot barbecue and cook for 4 minutes on each side, or until the flesh is firm.

Mix all the salsa ingredients and serve with the warm fish straight from the barbecue.

For red mullet & basil oil, place 4 gutted and scaled red mullet on a medium-hot barbecue with a little seasoning and a touch of olive oil and cook for 3 minutes on each side, or until the flesh is firm. Place a large handful of basil, 1 garlic clove, ⅓ cup pine nuts, and 5 tablespoons olive oil in a food processor and blend until smooth. Serve with the barbecued fish.

lobster tails with tarragon dressing

Serves **4**
Preparation time **4 minutes**
Cooking time **16–21 minutes**

1 teaspoon **Dijon mustard**
2 tablespoons **white wine vinegar**
6 tablespoons **olive oil**
3 tablespoons chopped **tarragon**
4 **raw lobster tails**

Place the mustard, vinegar, and oil in a small bowl and beat to combine. Stir in the tarragon and season with salt and pepper.

Place the lobster tails on a medium-hot barbecue, flesh-side down and cook for 6 minutes. Turn the tails over and spoon 1 tablespoon of dressing over the flesh of each lobster, then cook for an additional 10–15 minutes, or until cooked through. This is best done with the lid of the barbecue down if you have one.

Serve the lobster tails with the remaining dressing.

For classic thousand island dressing, to serve as an accompaniment, mix together 6 tablespoons mayonnaise, 1 tablespoon tomato ketchup, ½ teaspoon Worcestershire sauce, a squeeze of lemon juice, a pinch of cayenne pepper, 1 red and 1 yellow bell pepper, cored, seeded, and finely diced, and 1 tablespoon finely chopped chives. Season with salt and pepper.

index

acknowledgments

Executive editor: Nicky Hill
Senior editor: Lisa John
Deputy art director: Geoff Fennell
Designer: Sue Michniewicz
Photographer: David Munns
Food stylist: Marina Filippelli
Props stylist: Liz Hippisley
Production controller: Carolin Stransky

Special photography: © Octopus Publishing Grou
Limited/David Munns
Other photography: © Octopus Publishing Group
Limited 23, 27, 109, 225; /Stephen Conroy 6, 16, 21
31, 35, 39, 43, 47, 53, 57, 91, 133, 159, 167, 173, 17
191, 195, 199, 203, 207, 215, 217; /Lis Parsons 97,
211; /Gareth Sambidge 157, 163, 169; /Ian Wallace
179, 183, 187